AFRO-AMERICANS IN CALIFORNIA

AFRO-AMERICANS IN CALIFORNIA

SECOND EDITION

Rudolph M. Lapp
College of San Mateo

series editors:
Norris Hundley, jr.
John A. Schutz

Boyd & Fraser Publishing Company
San Francisco

AFRO-AMERICANS IN CALIFORNIA
Second edition
Rudolph M. Lapp

Manufactured in the United States of America

ISBN 0-87835-152-3

1 2 3 4 5 · 0 9 8 7 6

EDITORS' INTRODUCTION

MENTION THE NAME CALIFORNIA and the popular mind conjures up images of romance and adventure of the sort that prompted the Spaniards in the 1540s to name the locale after a legendary Amazon queen. State of mind no less than geographic entity, California has become a popular image of a wonderful land of easy wealth, good health, pleasant living, and unlimited opportunities. While this has been true for some, for others it has been a land of disillusionment, and for too many it has become a place of crowded cities, congested roadways, smog, noise, racial unrest, and other problems. Still, the romantic image has persisted to make California the most populated state in the Union and the home of more newcomers each year than came during the first three hundred years following discovery by Europeans.

For most of its history California has been shrouded in mystery, better known for its terrain than for its settlers — first the Indians who arrived at least 11,000 years ago and then the Spaniards who followed in 1769. Spaniards, Mexicans, and blacks added only slightly to the non-Indian population until the American conquest of 1846 ushered in an era of unparalleled growth. With the discovery of gold, the building of the transcontinental railroad, and the development of crops and cities, people in massive numbers from all parts of the world began to inhabit the region. Thus California became a land of newcomers where a rich mixture of cultures pervades.

Fact and fiction are intertwined so well into the state's traditions and folklore that they are sometimes difficult to separate. But close scrutiny reveals that the people of California have made many solid contributions in land and water use, conservation of resources, politics, education, transportation, labor organization, literature, architectural styles, and learning to live with people of different cultural and ethnic heritages. These contributions, as well as those instances when Californians performed less admirably, are woven into the design of the Golden State Series. The volumes in the Series are meant to be suggestive rather than exhaustive, interpretive rather than definitive. They invite the general public, the student, the scholar, and the teacher to read them not only for digested materials from a wide range of recent scholarship, but also for some new insights and ways of perceiving old problems. The Series, we trust, will be only the beginning of each reader's inquiry into the past of a state rich in historical excitement and significant in its impact on the nation.

Norris Hundley, jr.
John A. Schutz

For Pat
with love

CONTENTS

CHAPTER ONE

A Place in the Sun: The 1840s and 1850s

ACASUAL WALK on Broadway in downtown Los Angeles or Market Street in San Francisco will reveal a major aspect of California life — its ethnic composition. Probably nowhere in the world will more nationalities and ethnic groups walk side by side on their way to work or market than in those cities. The shades of white, black, brown, and yellow make for a mix of cultures and languages that astonishes visitors. From 1781 Los Angeles has had an Hispanic population with a sprinkling of blacks in it. Even earlier, San Francisco and San Jose experienced a similar mix. The coming of blacks to California and their settlement here was one part of the westward movement of Hispanic and Anglo peoples from the 1500s to the present, a movement which includes exploring the countryside, founding cities, breaking the soil, raising families, earning a living, founding churches. Blacks were always part of this migration, and today they represent one of California's significant racial groups. Their experiences are often the same as other ethnic groups', but they have also a unique history shaped by problems of racial abuse and segregation. In their history they have a governor, several mayors, assemblymen, and a great number of city dwellers who work in the professions as well as as postal carriers, clerks, and businessmen and women. They also have unemployed in large numbers; they have ghettos and have experienced other types of segregation.

Spanish colonial expansion forcibly brought Africans into the New World and started them on their first steps toward California. The sixteenth-century exploratory voyages of the Spanish took innumerable blacks to the New World as members of the crews. Estevanico, or Black Stephen, is the best known of these newcomers. His wanderings with Cabeza de Vaca in the Mississippi Valley and the Southwest are part of that region's history. Their description of the land led to its exploration by Francisco Vásquez de Coronado in 1541. Less glamorous, but of greater importance in this early period, was the arrival of increasing numbers of slaves to Mexico, then called New Spain. They became an important ingredient in the Spanish founding of Baja California in the seventeenth century, and in the eighteenth century, no longer as slaves, they helped settle Los Angeles in 1781 as farmers. Following the pattern of their Mexican experience, they lost their identity as Afro-Americans in California through the process of intermarriage with Indian and Spanish peoples. By the third decade of the nineteenth century Afro-Americans in California were identifying themselves as Mexicans, including such prominent families as Tapia and Pico who were known for their African forebears. [1]

During California's Mexican period, roughly the twenty-five years after 1821, the first known Afro-Americans arrived from the United States. They were often men of the sea who sailed into the Pacific area as crews on commercial vessels, mostly whalers from New England. They were a handful in number, and like their white counterparts, most were probably deserters who jumped ship to pursue an agreeable life in Mexican California. What could not have been more than several dozen black men were scattered throughout California and melted quickly into the general population. The best known was Allen B. Light, a former seaman who, after he integrated into California society by joining first the Catholic church (an absolute requirement for black or white) and marrying then a local woman, became an official responsible for suppressing the illegal otter hunting along the Santa Barbara Coast. [2]

Another prominent Afro-American immigrant of this period was Alexander Leidesdorff, whose African ancestry was unknown until after his death in 1848. This maritime merchant of Danish and West Indian black ancestry first went into business as a white man in New Orleans and then journeyed in 1841 to San Francisco, where he resumed his career as an export-import merchant. He also took a leading role in San Francisco's community life and was a central force in starting schools for children.[3] Further evidence that he was not known as an Afro-American was his appointment as a vice-consul for the United States by President James K. Polk, a southerner, just prior to the American occupation of California in 1846. Jacob W. Harlan, an Indianan who migrated to California before the gold rush, became well acquainted with Leidesdorff. Many years later, and long after he and others learned of Leidesdorff's black ancestry, Harlan wrote, "He was a good and fair man and a good citizen. . . . Instead of having his name given to the little street which bears it, he deserved to have one of the chief streets named for him."[4]

American occupation brought many newcomers to California and with them additional blacks. Military officers of southern origin took along their servants, who may have been their slaves as well. Even the famed northern general of the Civil War, William Tecumseh Sherman, brought a black man to Monterey as a servant in 1847. Government officials did likewise and, when the wives of these military and government personnel arrived, they frequently had black servants. One available statistic tells us that by 1847 there were ten blacks in San Francisco and fewer than ten in Monterey, which was still the center of northern California's social and political life.[5] Arriving monthly were also black servants of both sexes who came with the business and professional men who were seeking commercial opportunities in the West and needed help in setting up their enterprises.

In the black experience east of the Mississippi River there were periods of free black migration to the various western frontiers during the pre-gold-rush years, but these migrations did not signify large movements of people. Legislation in the free states at that time discouraged the migration of blacks to the West. For free blacks to migrate to western slave states would suggest they were uninformed. There is little indication that this ever happened. Abolitionists and Afro-American newspapers in the East kept blacks — at least those approximately fifty percent who were literate and who had access to the relatively few black papers — fully informed about racial prejudice in western free states. When California became part of the United States, these journals indicated that this new territory would be equally uninviting for people of color. Some editors even predicted that the new territory would be a slave state, an opinion they finally had to drop when California was admitted as a state in 1850.

But politics changed in January 1848 when gold was discovered on the American River. Within a few months northern California was ablaze with excitement. For a brief period San Francisco and Monterey were ghost towns as men hastened to the gold fields. Since both ports were now part of the United States, many commercial ships flying the stars and stripes stopped at those towns. When their crews heard stories of the gold, the vessels rapidly became ghost ships. There were scores, or perhaps hundreds, of free blacks among these crews, especially aboard the New England whalers. The census of 1860 reveals that there were 279 black men in Massachusetts alone classified as mariners. The cooks and stewards were always black men.[6] Most of these seamen headed quickly for the Mother Lode country along with their white compatriots. There were a few blacks associated with army and navy contingents who preceded the eastern black seamen into the gold fields, but the latter constituted the largest group of black gold miners.

News of the dramatic discovery of gold soon reached the eastern states, Latin America, and Europe, and the excitement brought on the 1849 gold rush. Blacks were part of that remarkable migration. Coastal city free blacks, many from Massachusetts as well as New York, Pennsylvania, and Maryland, traveled largely by the Panama route and some around Cape Horn to California. From the upper Mississippi Valley states many earned their way as employees of the overland groups. From the slave states hundreds of blacks accompanied their gold-hunting masters. Some came with a promise of freedom in California if the rewards of mining were great enough. Most welcomed the adventure. By 1850 there were 962 Afro-Americans in Cali

"Andy at the Sluice." A photo taken at the Auburn ravine in 1852. (*Reprinted by permission of the Bancroft Library, University of California, Berkeley.*)

fornia, predominantly in the Mother Lode counties, probably about half of them slaves.[7]

During the 1849–1850 gold rush blacks remained scattered and enjoyed very little community life. Still, there were those blacks of the free Negro communities of the northern states who regarded California more as an opportunity for profitable business and employment than as a place for successful gold mining. Mifflin Wistar Gibbs, the Philadelphia black abolitionist, is an example. Shortly after his arrival in San Francisco, he formed a partnership with a fellow black Philadelphian in a boot and shoe business that prospered.

Early in 1849 most gold seekers wanted California to become a free state. While the area's new laws reflected national racist attitudes, there was a widespread belief that California provided economic possibilities to everyone. Even the black and abolitionist press reported blacks doing well in the West. For instance, the Philadelphia black community read in their local antislavery paper that two blacks had returned home in 1851 with $30,000 after only four months in the diggings. Similar reports drew other free blacks in modest numbers to California, and by 1852 more than two thousand Afro-Americans were living in the state. Most of them were engaged in service or labor occupations, and a few had their own businesses. They congregated primarily in San Francisco, Sacramento, Marysville, and Stockton, in that order.

Southern California during the gold-rush decade grew much more slowly than northern California, but it held its population in spite of attractions elsewhere. A handful of blacks could be found scattered throughout this southern region with a half dozen residing in Los Angeles. They were engaged in various menial and farming occupations. Illustrative of the Afro-Americans who would eventually achieve standing in Los Angeles were Peter Biggs, who had a booming business as a barber; Biddy Mason, who won her freedom in a celebrated court case; and Robert Owens, whose subsequent material success in real estate gave the name "Owens Block" to property at Broadway near Third Street. However, black institutions in southern California would not become clearly visible until the end of the century.

In northern California churches were the first black organizations to develop. By 1852, San Francisco had both black Methodist and Baptist churches. Perhaps the first black church to be organized anywhere in California was the one founded in Sacramento by the Fletcher brothers, Barney and George, who were local merchants. They established an African Methodist Episcopal church. While some blacks attended the major white churches, the deep urge for independence in religious matters brought the overwhelming majority of Afro-Americans to form their own congregations. This wish for independence had its roots in the work of Richard Allen, a black preacher in Philadelphia. Shortly after the American Revolution he paved the way for institutional independence in religion for blacks and became the founder of the African Methodist Episcopal Church (A.M.E.). Blacks from the North tended to be members of A.M.E. churches, while blacks from the South gravitated towards the Baptist.

In the 1850s, the black population in California was overwhelmingly male, but family life gradually developed and by 1854 young black children were entering school. In San Francisco the African Methodist Episcopal Church founded its own school, and in Sacramento a private community school was set up by some black families. California state government at this time did little for any school children and nothing for blacks. Then, toward the end of the decade, the legislature allowed counties and cities to use tax funds for segregated schools. By that time church basement schools could be found in Marysville and Stockton as well. The teachers in the early years were usually A.M.E. and black Baptist clergymen. Among them were such accomplished men as the New Bedford–born Jeremiah B. Sanderson, who had struggled successfully for integrated education in his native Massachusetts. The struggle in California for integrated schools continued to be opposed by authorities and the press even after the conclusion of the Civil War. Only in the 1870s were the efforts of blacks and reformers rewarded with success.[8]

While many blacks, as well as whites, remained gold miners until the end of the 1850s, the centers of economic and social life soon became the four major cities of northern California. It was here that employment and material accumulation were possible in a significant way. By the middle of this decade there were scores of blacks in successful businesses and trades. A great number of blacks worked as seamen, cooks, stewards, and in occupations related to food and service employment. The ever-increasing shipping and passenger traffic of San Francisco Bay was a source of much black income. Many also found work in a great variety of menial occupations. Afro-Americans in California were thus matching, if not exceeding, the wealth of their counterparts in the eastern states. As propertied persons, they were increasingly concerned about the laws protecting their property as well as their persons. But California's laws fell short of their needs.

Like the constitutions of many free states, California's 1849 constitution, and the laws passed under it, did not provide blacks with either the vote or the right to testify in court. The denial of equal testimony rights was the most offensive of the state's laws. As passed in 1850, it read that: "No black or mulatto person or Indian shall be permitted to give evidence in favor of or against any white person. Every person who shall have one eighth part or more of Negro blood shall be deemed a mulatto, and every person who shall have one half Indian blood shall be deemed an Indian." This latter discrimination was most threatening to black property rights as well as to personal safety. If blacks were robbed by white persons, and if there were only black witnesses, no matter how many, and no willing white witnesses, the injured blacks had no recourse to the law. Mifflin Wistar Gibbs, the black tradesman of San Francisco, was among those victimized by this law. He and his partner were robbed in broad daylight in their shop when two whites took a pair of expensive boots and walked off laughing. This unjust statute became the spur to the most sustained black civil rights struggle of the 1850s. It produced the California Colored Convention movement and three petition campaigns to amend the state's testimony law.[9]

Experienced black leadership in the struggle for equal testimony rights was readily available. Many of the transplanted black easterners, while all quite young, had been leaders in the abolitionist movement, in the state colored convention movements, and in their churches. The roster included men such as William H. Hall, William H. Yates, Peter Anderson, Jonas H. Townsend, Henry Collins, Mifflin W. Gibbs, and ministers T. M. D. Ward, John J. Moore, and Jeremiah B. Sanderson. Gibbs later held responsible public office in post–Civil War Republican administrations. Younger men, such as Edward Duplex from New Haven, Connecticut, rose rapidly into the California black leadership class. These men had been often associated with Frederick Douglass and William Lloyd Garrison in eastern struggles for black rights. They were articulate and educated and made good use of the college training they had at such institutions as Oberlin College in Ohio.

Some of these black settlers of San Francisco organized in 1852 a Franchise League, the initial force in the struggle for equal rights in offering court testimony. They and blacks from Sacramento conducted a petition campaign that was ignored by the Democrats who controlled the state legislature. Between 1852 and 1855 the black community continued to grow by migration, and the number of leaders increased as well. In 1855 there was another effort to revise the testimony laws. That year as well the American (Know Nothing) party won the state elections, including the governorship. Among the party's leaders were individuals whom blacks considered friends of their cause. The increasing black interest in politics led in November 1855 to the First California Colored Convention, a statewide gathering that took place in Sacramento and reflected the convention movement already under way in some eastern states.

This three-day conference agreed on an energetic petition campaign that would concentrate on white supporters and on appeals for justice for the highly literate black minority. Other subjects reached the convention floor, but the delegates felt that the right to offer testimony was more important in their present plans than suffrage or education. Discussion about a black weekly newspaper also arose, but action was postponed. (The debate resulted in the founding during the next year of the *Mirror of the Times.*) The petition committees gathered thousands of signatures, but they were rejected by a disinterested legislature. Despite the rebuff, the convention executive committee agreed to call another conference. [10]

In December 1856 the Second Colored Convention met, and again in Sacramento. It had been heralded in September by the appearance of California's first black weekly newspaper, the *Mirror of the Times.* As the official organ of the convention movement, the weekly was edited by William H. Newby and Jonas Townsend. (About fifty or sixty issues were published before the newspaper expired in January 1858. Only three numbers are known to exist today.) Newby was a Virginian, a freeborn Negro who was a regular correspondent to the *Frederick Douglass Paper,* and Jonas Townsend had edited a Negro newspaper in New York. Financial support of the *Mirror* was an important topic of the second convention, but the delegates' main concern continued to be the fight for equal testimony rights. A second petition campaign was mounted, but it too was rejected by the state legislature, although a bit more politely. This campaign was marked by an awkward problem that faced the black petitioners. The California constitution denied equal testimony rights to Chinese and Indians as well as blacks. Many blacks knew that most of their white supporters would not push for testimony rights for Chinese and Indians, so they agitated only for their own group. The expression "third world solidarity" would not be heard until over a hundred years later.

The events of 1857 did not heighten the spirit of the California black community as far as civil rights were concerned. Nationally the decision in *Dred Scott* v. *Sandford* was handed down by the U.S. Supreme Court; in California the blacks' petition campaign was rejected a second time; and in state politics, Governor J. Neely Johnson was defeated at the polls. These serious setbacks left black leaders with no clear alternative but to schedule a third convention which would meet in San Francisco early in October.

They then set an agenda for the convention which included the continuation of the petition campaign to democratize the testimony laws, a plan to find financial support for the *Mirror of the Times,* and a report on the lack of educational opportunities for black children. These issues and others, all reflecting the continued growth in numbers of the black community, were to receive major attention in 1858, but other, more threatening concerns now pressed on them. The state legislature unexpectedly introduced an antiblack migration bill containing vicious and humiliating provisions which reflected the emotion generated from California's most famous fugitive slave case.

The Archy Lee trial in 1858 stands apart from other fugitive slave cases in California. Before state voters had outlawed slavery in the 1849 constitution, hundreds of blacks had been brought by their masters to the state in order to mine gold. When the antislavery provision of the constitution became known, some masters had already returned to the South with their slaves; others continued to come, feeling certain that nothing would happen to their "property." Still others came with slaves to whom they promised freedom after a certain amount of gold had been dug, usually $2,000 worth. It was not long before a few blacks took matters into their own hands and fled to freedom within the boundaries of this free state. When they were recaptured, the courts entered the controversy. Some judges freed blacks, stating that the national Fugitive Slave Law of 1850 did not apply to those who fled slavery within California's boundaries. This prompted the state legislature, which sympathized with slave owners, to pass a temporary fugitive slave law ensuring possession of "slaves to owners returning to the southern states." The new law was passed in 1852 and was renewed annually until 1856, when it was allowed

" A R C H Y . "

TO THE FRIENDS

......OF THE......

CONSTITUTION AND LAWS.

THE COMMITTEE APPOINTED BY THE
Colored People having expended a large amount, and in-
curred heavy obligations in prosecuting and defending the case
in the Courts of Sacramento, Stockton and San Francisco, and
believing the principles to be vindicated are those which should
interest all lovers of right and justice, independent of com-
plexion, respectfully solicit contributions for this object, which
will be faithfully appropriated, if left with

m20-3t   E. J. JOHNSON, 184 Clay street.

"Archy." An advertisement in the *California Chronicle*, San Francisco, 1858.

to expire. In January 1858, a young Mississippian named
Charles Stovall brought his family slave, Archy Lee, to Sacramento. Eighteen-year-old Lee, influenced by activist free blacks
in the town, struck for freedom. He was shortly apprehended,
and for four months, from January to April 1858, the state was
aroused by the struggle conducted by the black community and
its white allies to free Archy Lee. What made the case atypical
was the state supreme court's decision, in spite of the law, to
return Lee to slavery because his owner was "young and inexperienced"! Local newspapers as well as those in the East ridi-
culed the ruling of California's supreme court.

The case became even more dramatic as Lee's supporters organized to save him. An effort by Stovall to get Lee out of
the state unnoticed was frustrated in San Francisco Bay. This
occurred because influential newspapers and political leaders
believed the state supreme court's decision to be unjust. As a

consequence Lee's supporters were able to resume his fight in the more favorable courts of San Francisco. The final phase of the case took place before the United States Commissioner in San Francisco. This southern-born federal appointee, William Penn Johnston, received the case because strong antislavery legal aid had obstructed Stovall in San Francisco courts. Stovall's last hope was that this southerner would interpret the federal Fugitive Slave Law of 1850 as legal justification for returning Archy Lee to slavery. Johnston certainly knew in advance that the case did not come under his jurisdiction but, undoubtedly for political reasons, he agreed to hear it. After weeks of courtroom drama, the commissioner declared that the Fugitive Slave Law did not apply to Archy Lee because he had not crossed state lines in his flight from slavery. Archy Lee went free and into the arms of a tumultuously happy crowd of supporters. [11]

The Archy Lee case aroused some state legislators who almost passed a bill to ban black immigration in 1858. The case also deflected to some extent the work of the Third Colored Convention. Blacks became so involved in the details and excitement of the Archy Lee case that the petition campaign for equal testimony rights suffered. Black leaders, moreover, failed to anticipate the amount of hostility that would be aroused. Though they were able to gather many names for the petition, the state legislature rejected it for a third time.

These defeats one after another obviously discouraged blacks who were concerned about the success of holding a fourth colored convention. The Republican party, which nationally contained the most friends of blacks, was still quite small in California. The few covert allies whom blacks had in the Democratic party were deeply embroiled in inner-party rivalries. Though the Archy Lee victory in 1858 delighted blacks, it also raised problems.

Some blacks now used the opportunity of a gold rush to Canada's Fraser River Valley to leave California. Also, business and job opportunities in British Columbia, especially in Victoria, as well as the promise of dignity and respect in the Queen's colony, provided an escape from the realities of California life. Those leaving included many who were economically well off but anxious for a less racist atmosphere. The records suggest that most of these migrants did well in their occupations, and some, such as Mifflin Wistar Gibbs, eventually held elected offices in Victoria. When the Civil War began in 1861, a few returned to California and even to the eastern states.

The departure of the migrants to Canada did not seriously change the number of blacks in California. By 1860, there were still nearly five thousand Afro-Americans, some of them West Indians, mainly in the larger cities of northern California. In 1859, the silver discoveries in Nevada attracted a few blacks to that area, and in the 1860s other discoveries there drew additional blacks. These migrations only slightly affected the numbers of blacks and just a trickle settled in California during the Civil War, thus accounting for their relative stability in population in the 1860s.

During the Civil War western blacks participated as an integral part in the economic life of the region. As members of a minority group, they suffered from civil rights discrimination and cultural oppression, but economically they were comfortable. Discrimination in California at this time was concentrated against the Indians and the Chinese, by far the larger minority groups. Blacks were still but one percent of the state's population. A thousand resided in San Francisco, where they tended to live in the older parts of town, most noticeably in the area south of Telegraph Hill, in a mixed community of Anglos and Hispanics. By 1860 the second largest black population resided in Sacramento and numbered over four hundred. It was also in an unsegregated community of lower-income groups with the Chinese most vividly the other people of color. There were at this time only two additional black communities of any significance and organization, and they were in Marysville and Stockton. The former had slightly more than a hundred black residents and the latter slightly less. Here again, these people lived in unsegregated but poor areas in the cities.

When actual fighting between the North and the South broke out in April 1861, there was a surge of hope among blacks in the North that slavery was doomed and their position in American life would be immediately improved. But Abraham Lincoln's emphasis upon union instead of abolition in the early years of the war was disappointing. He assured the South that he had no intention of impairing slavery where it already existed, and the United States Army rejected free blacks who wished to enlist in the war against the South. These actions dashed the hopes of northern blacks and, during the latter part of 1861 and the first half of 1862, their mood was pessimistic. Black public opinion in California did not become clear until the founding of the *Appeal* in 1862, the successor to the *Mirror of the Times.* The birth of the *Appeal* was primarily due to the presence of Phillip A. Bell, a talented black journalist who came to California in 1860, and Peter Anderson, a leader in the California Colored Convention movement. Until publication of the *Appeal,* the only hint of black public opinion on the war and the election of Lincoln is the existence of a petition signed by several hundred black Californians requesting help to leave the United States. The petitioners declared that American blacks found little hope for their future in the nation. Whether this petition was a symbolic protest or expressed a genuine desire to emigrate will probably never be known.

If the *Appeal* accurately reflected California black opinion about the Civil War, then Afro-Americans agreed with Frederick Douglass, the great black abolitionist leader in the East, who assumed that only good would result from the use of arms against the Confederacy. The *Appeal* kept up a running commentary on the desirability of recruiting black troops and quoted leading white suporters of this view. During these years California was not asked to send troops to the eastern war zones and instead was given the responsibility of manning the abandoned western forts and guarding the silver transported from Nevada. In 1863, the Union government even exempted California from the draft of that year.

However, there were California blacks who by 1863 wished to participate in the eastern military struggle. Efforts in this direction, while received politely in Washington, never resulted in the creation of California black companies. A few western blacks did enlist in black companies in the East through their own efforts, and some others enlisted in California companies which remained in the West. At least twenty-six black men in eight different companies were in uniform, all of them performing culinary duties. [12]

The first sign of enthusiasm for the war among California

blacks occurred in April 1862 when Congress freed the blacks
in Washington, D.C., by the method of compensated emancipation — paying the masters to free their slaves. Celebrations
quickly followed in the San Francisco black community. Soon,
while making it clear they felt that slavery itself still needed a
frontal attack, blacks in their churches as well as in their public
meetings raised funds to care for wounded Union soldiers. When
the Emancipation Proclamation of 1863 became a certainty,
blacks dropped their cautious reserve toward the war. They had
long observed the anniversary of the British Emancipation Act
while doing little about July Fourth. But when the Emancipation Proclamation became a fact, grand events were promoted
in the major black population centers. Even though they were
not invited to participate in established July Fourth celebrations, they planned events of their own, stating clearly for the
first time that they felt they were becoming an accepted part of
the nation.

The Emancipation Proclamation evoked the most elaborate
and joyous gathering of blacks yet seen in San Francisco. Their
support of the war then accelerated. The Sanitary Fund, fore-
runner of the Red Cross and spearheaded in California by
Unitarian minister Thomas Starr King, benefited from Afro-
American enthusiasm. King, who at all times after his arrival
in California in 1860 showed friendship to the blacks, was
grateful for the hundreds of dollars they had raised for the
Sanitary Fund. By 1864, enthusiasm for Lincoln had reached
the point where San Francisco blacks, although still without
the vote, held a mass meeting and nominated him symbolically
for a second term as President. By 1865, racism had ebbed
sufficiently in San Francisco for the city's black community to
be invited officially to participate in the Fourth of July parade.
Afro-Americans in other California communities received mixed
treatment in this regard.

In local matters the Civil War period was an uneven story of
gains and setbacks for California blacks. While racist attitudes
were perhaps as strong as ever among the majority of whites,
discrimination experienced a temporary decline and was some-
what muted during the years of civil combat. These were the
years of the governorships of Leland Stanford (1862–1863), a
Republican, and Frederic F. Low (1863–1867), a Union Repub-

lican. In 1863, the onerous testimony law was finally democratized to the extent that at least blacks could testify with full equality. Indians and Chinese were still denied this benefit. Contemporary observers, both black and white, commented on the general economic well-being of blacks and the existence of some who were well-to-do. But serious problems remained in the area of education. From a few dozen the black population of children in the state had grown to several hundred, especially in San Francisco and Sacramento. As they multiplied, black parents became interested in ways to improve the education of their children.

While there appeared to be no complaint about the fact that black teachers in California and even white teachers in black schools received less salary than white teachers in white schools, blacks were concerned about good schools for their children. Contemporary descriptions leave little doubt that most classrooms and other facilities were inferior to the accommodations provided white children. Furthermore, high schools were virtually barred to black children. An 1862 report to the San Francisco Board of Education about a black schoolroom noted that

> it is a basement and below the grade of the street. It is badly ventilated — the air from the west and north sides comes laden with the effluvia of cellars, sinks and vaults contiguous, and is foul and unhealthful. . . . The hall above the school room is occupied by a military company. The loud sounds arising from their exercises, at times, greatly disturb those of the schoolroom. The plastering is broken and falling from the ceiling, and the water from above runs through the floor upon the desks and floor of the schoolroom beneath.

In the 1860s more and more black children reached high school age at a time when admission to higher education was denied them. San Francisco blacks valiantly worked to establish a private black high school, the Livingstone Institute, but this facility lasted only a decade. Integration eventually opened high schools to blacks, but not until 1890, through the Wysinger case in Visalia, did the last vestiges of high school segregation end.[13]

San Francisco blacks in the 1860s also struggled to achieve equal access to the city's railways. Two instances of ejection of black passengers were successfully fought in the local courts with damage awards in each case, but these awards did not end discrimination by the city's lines. After the Civil War, the best known incident involved the legendary Mary Ellen (Mammy) Pleasant. She had hailed the conductor, who disregarded her and failed to stop. "We don't take colored people in these cars," he later told her. She fought her grievance to the state supreme court and won a damage award of $500. As late as 1870, one of the city's lines again ejected a black woman passenger, and the courts again awarded damages.

Though these cases had importance for Afro-Americans, emotions were most aroused by the struggle over the right to vote. Blacks raised that issue frequently in the pages of the *Appeal*. By 1865, at the time of the Fourth Colored Convention, black public opinion had crystallized to the point of readiness. The convention took place in Sacramento in October and had the help of a second black weekly. Phillip Bell, having had a falling out with Peter Anderson, left the *Appeal* and began publishing the *Elevator*. Personalities rather than issues caused this split, and the dangers of an emotional confrontation at the convention threatened the movement. The two men and their followers suspended their rivalry briefly that year to share publicly their common grief over the assassination of Abraham Lincoln.

The concerns of the fourth convention vividly reflected changing times. The first three conventions—in 1855, 1856, and 1857—had focused almost exclusively on the right of equal testimony in the state courts. In 1863, when this right had been won, Afro-American leaders demanded recognition of the black right to vote. Emotion mounted rapidly, and by 1865 this demand had become a burning issue for blacks and many whites as well. At the convention in Sacramento speech after speech urged the justice of the black man's claim to the franchise and its validity as a right based on his religion, his contributions to American life, and, more pointedly, his participation in the Union army. Other issues were also discussed. Education received more attention than at prior conventions, reflecting the growth in numbers of black school-age children. Interest in the building of the transcontinental railroad was expressed by many delegates who called for the employment of 20,000 ex-slaves to work on its construction. Whether these blacks would have welcomed such work will never be known.

Again the resolutions of this latest convention were not heard favorably by the state legislature. The railroad would be built by Chinese and Irish labor, and the demand of California's Afro-Americans for the right to vote was ignored by the 1865 California Union (Republican) state convention. Nonetheless, the blacks in San Francisco could feel that there was some goodwill still available to them. The city in 1865 officially invited them for the first time to participate in the Fourth of July festivities. The blacks prepared lavishly and enthusiastically. In 1866, the invitation was not repeated, however, because the political climate during that single year had moved to the right on racial issues. Henry H. Haight, a former Republican now turned Democrat, had become governor. He was hostile to blacks as voters, and his followers in the state legislature shared his attitude. The lawmakers refused to give blacks (not to mention Indians and Chinese) the vote, and blacks had to wait until passage of the Fifteenth Amendment in 1870 before they obtained the franchise. The fact that the right to vote was given to California blacks by the Congress of the United States instead of the state contributed to the general sentiment by blacks that their hopes could always be better realized at the national level rather than at the state level. The next hundred years would only strengthen this attitude.

Black activities in southern California lagged behind those in the northern half during the first decades of statehood. Although the early settlers of Los Angeles were of mixed ancestry, with the passage of time the importance of the African element in their heritage lessened. The descendants of these settlers considered themselves Mexicans.[14] During the era of the gold rush individual blacks of United States origin worked and lived in widely scattered locations in the sparsely settled region south of the Tehachapis, with only a handful residing in Los Angeles.

This small group of blacks, living in an environment dominated in the 1850s and 1860s by Americans from the southern states, produced some notable individuals. The best-known personality of those decades was Biddy Mason, an ex-slave who in 1855 battled her Mormon master for her freedom and gained it for herself and her family as well as another family of slaves. The

Mormons, who had settled in San Bernardino and then left en masse in 1858, had slaves with them who were given the option of remaining in California. Most of them remained and eventually entered the small Los Angeles community of free blacks. Biddy Mason, through hard work, became a property owner of some importance in Los Angeles, as did the black Owens family, into which members of the Mason family later married. The coming together through marriage of these two families brought the Owens's descendants financial resources that made them, by the turn of the century, among the most prosperous, if not the most prosperous, black family in Los Angeles.

Not as wealthy, but well known, was a black barber and "character" named Peter Biggs. He gained much notoriety during the Civil War as a black who favored Jefferson Davis over Abraham Lincoln. However, during those early years, there were too few Afro-Americans in southern California to establish a significant community life, although Mason was reportedly holding religious services in her home for interested blacks. Life for black and white alike moved at a slow pace in the southern part of the state and reflected the pastoral setting. Afro-Americans experienced a growth in numbers that accelerated sharply near the end of the century with a general increase of population in southern California.[15]

In the first two decades of statehood, blacks remained few in number—4,086 or 1.46 percent of the population in 1860 and 4,272 or 1.15 percent in 1870. They had laid foundations of association, however, and a few were business people in the northern cities of California, while many throughout the state were property owners. By far the greatest numbers were engaged in the service and food trades as productive members of the expanding society. In the decades after the Civil War energetic white men of the most humble origin were able in California's dynamic economy to attain great wealth and corporate power. Blacks of equal ability, however, could not reach these heights in California or elsewhere in the nation for many reasons—certainly race prejudice was of central importance.

CHAPTER TWO

New Struggles in the Gilded Age

B ETWEEN 1860 and 1900, the black population of California gradually increased. The number in 1860 was about five thousand, although the official census (which invariably overlooked many blacks) placed the number closer to four thousand. The 1880 census gives a figure of 6,018. Most of these Americans were still of the gold-rush generation, but there is evidence suggesting that some ex-slaves migrated to California after the Civil War. While the Radical Reconstruction period, which began in 1867, fostered hope among blacks in the former slave states, the passing years also brought much turmoil and suffering. To escape their fate, blacks made their way to California. The press gives a few clues about this small migration, especially in its occasional observations that cotton was being raised in the San Joaquin Valley and that ex-slaves were being brought out to do the work. Other brief notes refer to "freedmen" as members of the laboring force.[1] As of 1880, most blacks were still living in northern California. San Francisco had 1,628 Afro-Americans as compared to Los Angeles's 188. Fast-growing Alameda County across the Bay from San Francisco had 686. While all but two counties in 1880 recorded black residents, the numbers were small.

Although the Democrat-controlled politics of the state were either indifferent or hostile to black interests, national Republican administrations were still sufficiently positive that blacks felt encouraged to participate in civil rights activities. The relative economic security of many blacks also served as an inducement and support for such activities. Though Afro-Americans were still heavily employed in the service and food trades, employment was good. Some were active in gold mining, which had shifted from panning to quartz mining, and had organized independent black mining companies. The ex-slave Mose Rodgers gained the reputation of being an excellent hydraulic mining superintendent whose company operations in Mariposa County were prosperous. He was typical of the former slave who did well and who had the leisure to become a leader in the convention movement. [2]

In 1870, when California blacks finally won the vote through the Fifteenth Amendment to the U.S. Constitution, they measured their gains and decided to test the waters. High on their agenda was an examination of the distressing state of education for their children. Second-rate school facilities for black children, funded by local government and paid in part by taxes levied on black parents, irritated them. But they disliked the inequality of opportunity even more. It was clear that "separate" was never "equal," and insistence on school integration generated a parallel demand for proper funding. The law in 1871 provided for separate schools where there were ten or more black school-age children and for the admission of these children to the white-enrolled schools if they were fewer than ten and *if local whites did not object.* [3] They did, of course, and, consequently, black children were left with no schools in many rural areas. To remedy this situation a call was made for an "Educational Convention" to take place in Stockton in November 1871.

The Educational Convention met at the church of Jeremiah B. Sanderson, who was regarded as the most distinguished black pedagogue in California. The delegates decided first to ask the legislature to amend the state's educational code so as to halt the segregation of black children. The Chinese were not included in their request because the delegates felt that such a broadening of the campaign would ensure its defeat by those hostile to the Asians. A champion for the black cause was found in state Senator Seldon J. Finney of San Mateo County, who in

Tombstone of Louden Nelson in Evergreen Cemetery, Santa Cruz, California.
(*Photo by Patricia T. Lapp.*)

1871 introduced a bill to end segregation for Afro-American
children. When the bill met defeat the next year, the executive
committee of the Educational Convention turned to the courts
for help.

During the summer of 1872, black leaders prepared for the
court case by collecting money at meetings in San Francisco,
Sacramento, Stockton, and Marysville. (Contact at this time
with the small Los Angeles black community did not seem
worth the effort.) One of the most important achievements of
the black organizers was their success in obtaining the services
of a prominent lawyer, John W. Dwinelle, who had long held
sympathies for black causes.

The feelings that inspired this fresh surge of activity among blacks, especially those in San Francisco, can be understood from a description of the city's school facilities for black children. It appeared in the weekly Afro-American newspaper, the *Appeal*, on July 11, 1874:

> There has been no improvement made in the condition of the main school on Russian Hill, which resembles a picture of Noah's Ark landed on Mount Ararat, and the other, a small room rented by the Board of Education, in a dwelling house in the neighborhood of Fifth and Folsom streets. There are 43 or more splendidly built school houses in the city suited or adapted to every neighborhood, while colored children have to travel the two extremes of the city to gratify the prejudices of proscription.

Not surprisingly, the first opportunity for a court case on the desegregation issue occurred in San Francisco. The attempts of Mary Frances Ward, a young black girl, to enter the Broadway School were denied by school principal Noah Flood on the grounds that there was a "colored" school that she could attend. So began *Ward* v. *Flood,* which went all the way to the state supreme court.

Eighteen months later, in 1874, the court ruled that Mary Ward's rights had not been denied since there was an all-black school available to her. This ruling was an early enunciation of the separate but equal doctrine, which the U.S. Supreme Court would approve in 1896 in *Plessy* v. *Ferguson.* The *Ward* decision, however, differed slightly. In school districts where there was no school for black children (the law required no separate school for blacks if they numbered fewer than ten), the community was *compelled* to let the black children enroll in the white school.[4] For the first time such children living in the rural and less populated regions of California were able to get an elementary education. The decision did not come too soon. A professional teachers' organization in the state estimated that in 1874 one fourth of school-age black children were not in school.

Even before the *Ward* decision, the practice of segregating children was weakening. Oakland in 1872 permitted black children to enter the elementary schools with white children, and there were no difficulties. By the last half of the 1870s school districts everywhere were closing their segregated schools and enrolling black children in white schools. This often was done over the protests of racist-minded newspapers and local pressure groups. In San Francisco the principal argument in favor of integration was not grounded in the demand for equality but rather in the need to operate the schools economically. During the depression of the seventies the argument had great weight even with prejudiced whites.

When the Fifteenth Amendment in 1870 gave the vote to black males, California's Afro-Americans entered the political process for the first time. They registered in good numbers and prepared to vote for sympathetic candidates. Throughout the rest of the decade they backed, with only occasional waverings, Republicans. Any hesitations of loyalty occurred generally over issues that were close to California blacks on the local scene and only occasionally over national issues. With politics now open to them, blacks organized Republican clubs in communities where the talent was available. The largest of these clubs was in San Francisco where the hundreds of black voters had not yet appreciated the power of the swing vote between Republicans and Democrats. But even where their votes were not of such significance, blacks still remained keenly interested in politics and became members of Grant-Colfax clubs and Newton-Pacheco clubs. They joined, in the 1870s, Charles Sumner clubs in a quixotic effort to promote the presidential candidacy of that Massachusetts Republican senator who was the blacks' greatest national civil rights champion. Senator Sumner had introduced a civil rights bill, and California blacks pinned their hopes on this measure to achieve school integration. The bill became law in 1875, but the provisions for integrated education had been deleted due to lack of support by Republicans. (The U.S. Supreme Court would find the law unconstitutional in 1883.) Black loyalty to the regular Republicans is most evident in their rejection of the candidacy of the Republican bolter Horace Greeley, who had long been an opponent of slavery, but had joined the Democrats in opposing U. S. Grant.

In spite of their loyalty, California's black Republicans had their moments of doubt about the party of Lincoln, particularly when it became the party of Andrew Johnson and Ulysses Grant. They detected foot-dragging by state Republicans before 1870 when blacks felt California should grant them the vote by state

From the SAN FRANCISCO DAILY EXAMINER, Aug. '69

Shall Negroes and Chinamen Vote in California?

READ!

AN ADDRESS

BY THE

DEMOCRATIC STATE CENTRAL COMMITTEE

TO THE VOTERS OF CALIFORNIA.

law. They found Republicans in the state admonishing blacks not to "push too fast" in school matters, and they got few jobs from the Republicans when the party had power to grant them. While most California blacks remained true to the Republican party, they had frankly no alternative party to join. There was little in the Democratic party of the post–Civil War decades to attract them.

During the years when the Chinese and railroad issues wracked California politics, blacks supported the Republican view. The Chinese question was particularly awkward for them; on the one hand, they deeply resented the hostility to the Chinese based on racist concepts, but, on the other, they were troubled by the big employers' (usually Republicans) preference for Chinese labor. To counter this, the black press, in an attempt to persuade employers to hire black labor, frequently emphasized that blacks were not only Americans, but also Christians and English-speaking. At the same time the black press was generally favorable to the railroad monopoly and the restraint of union activity.

Yet Republican loyalty did not make the Chinese labor issue and its threat to black employment disappear. Blacks in the food service occupations suffered under Chinese competition in the 1870s. The Chinese entry into the small business world evoked a longstanding lament from black journalist Phillip Bell. "Even the heathen 'Chinee'," he stated, ". . . get into some business, while our people are the only class that do not develope [sic] their business capacity."[5]

Without exception, the black press opposed the Irish-dominated Workingman's party of the seventies. It also opposed the 1879 state constitution, which had the support of the Workingmen's party. Rivalry between the Afro-American and Irish working-class communities had arisen out of job competition at the lowest rung of the labor ladder. This hostility originated in New England and New York and spread to the West Coast. The attitude of blacks toward unions is easy to understand since the emergence of unionism was so often associated with black exclusion from jobs.

Although a handful of blacks in San Francisco in the late 1870s were attracted to the anti-Chinese appeal of the Workingmen's party, and probably voted for its candidates in 1879, the majority black sentiment opposed essentially anything the party advocated. Black leader George Washington Dennis, Jr., the son of a slave who came to California during the gold rush and freed himself by self-purchase, wrote shortly after the 1879 convention that he opposed Chinese immigration but that the "instigators of this movement are a class of foreign dema-gogues . . . who own no property . . . [and] do not know the first letter of the alphabet. But by far the most disgusting part of it all is that some of our race should be found among this motley throng."[6]

The mood of this rivalry with the Irish must have reached Sacramento, but did not enter the deliberations of the Fifth State Colored Convention which assembled in November 1873. The convention, however, gave evidence of other developments in California's black communities. The number of delegates revealed that, while San Francisco and Sacramento remained the major centers of black life in the state, Stockton had moved ahead of Marysville to be third in importance. San Jose had emerged as a new center, and for the first time Los Angeles had representation. Also, an examination of the names of the dele-gates reveals the increased participation of ex-slaves, who had by now achieved relatively comfortable lives. Since *Ward* v. *Flood* was still pending before the state supreme court, the issue of education was very much on the minds of the delegates. The foot-dragging of the Republican party at the national level, where Senator Sumner's civil rights bill was having trouble, plus the evasiveness of the California Republicans over the efforts at integrated education in the state, raised criticism of the party among the delegates. Though a resolution to censure publicly the party was turned aside, rumblings of discontent continued. In spite of uncertain political support from whites, the convention delegates decided to press for integrated edu-cation.

From the 1880s to the end of the century, the growth of the black community was constant but meager, always hovering at one percent of the total population. The Chinese, Mexican, and Native American minority groups were still considerably larger. In 1880 the U.S. Census reported 6,018 blacks in California, and in 1900, 11,045. In the major cities of the state blacks were still predominantly in the service, food, and menial occupations. However, a few businessmen could be found in the larger urban centers, especially in San Francisco.

Little is known of the reasons for the slow growth of the California black population in the two decades immediately following the Civil War. A contemporary black westerner opined that many eastern blacks felt that it was dangerous to make the journey through unsettled country because of hostile Indians.[7] This impression of fear would be strong with eastern blacks because it was in the post–Civil War years that the all-black military units in the West were assigned to fighting Indians.

Basic research is scanty for the latter third of the century in western black history, but some facts are known. The near doubling of the state's black population by 1890 is explained by the real estate boom in southern California, which produced a black population gain in Los Angeles County from 188 in 1880 to 1,817 in 1890, a tenfold increase. In the same general area similar sharp increases took place. In 1880 the Fresno County black population was 40 and by 1890 it was 457. Even Kern County went from 4 to 130 in the period.

These statistics stand in contrast to the growth of the black communities in the northern part of the state. In San Francisco the increase was imperceptible, going from 1,628 in 1880 to 1,847 in 1890. The same was true for Oakland, where the figures were 686 in 1880 and 785 in 1890. In Sacramento County there was a small decline in the black population from 560 in 1880 to 513 in 1890. The number three and four counties in black population in the gold rush era, Yuba and San Joaquin, reflected different rates of growth between 1880 and 1890. In San Joaquin County, where there was some general growth of the white population, the number of blacks, chiefly in Stockton, rose from 328 in 1880 to 353 in 1890. In Yuba County, where the white population suffered a slight decline, blacks, mainly in Marysville, dropped in numbers from 247 in 1880 to 218 ten years later. Whether this decline represented stability or stagnation for the black community in Marysville is unknown. Perhaps the latter, for Marysville's best-known black citizen, Edward Duplex, had by then moved his barber shop to Wheatland in the southern end of the county.

Throughout the state the census records of rural counties for 1880 and 1890 reveal small growths and small declines of the

black population. In general terms, the northern counties of the
state showed most of the declines, but there were surprising
examples of growth in Santa Clara County, where the black
population rose from 54 in 1880 to 221 a decade later. In the
years after the gold rush there was a small but constant number
of black farmers, farm tenants, farm workers, and cowboys
(vaqueros) scattered throughout the state. In numbers, they
were usually less than a hundred in spite of considerable exhor-
tation by black leaders that more blacks should turn to agriculture. The still-fresh memory of slavery gave blacks a deep
aversion to working on the land. Brief attempts at cotton raising by white promoters in southern California resulted in the
rapid loss of their imported black labor shortly after arrival.
These Afro-Americans usually headed for Los Angeles, where
they found work as day laborers.

Some general reasons can be cited for the growth of the black
population in California. The coming of the railroads to the
West was very important since many of the railroad workers,
especially sleeping-car porters and "red caps," were black men.
Redcaps and Pullman porters were as familiar a sight to an older
generation as airline attendants are to today's airline passengers.
Many of these black railroad workers settled or retired with
their families in western cities. They and other black migrants
gradually introduced a new generation of western blacks who
replaced the generation of gold-rush Afro-Americans who were
now dead. In the 1880s and 1890s the older generation's two
newspapers, the *Pacific Appeal* and the *Elevator,* ceased publication and were replaced by other ventures into black journalism.

Another reason for the rapid growth of the southern California black community in comparison to its northern counter-
part was the greater expansion of trade unionism in the Bay
Area. The tragic practice in so many urban areas of unionized
white workers excluding blacks created deep hostility to unions
among blacks. In the turn-of-the-century decades unionism
made significant strides in San Francisco, but was deterred in
Los Angeles by powerful antiunion sentiment among employers
led by Harrison Gray Otis, publisher of the *Los Angeles Times.*
Typical of San Francisco is the case of the Palace Hotel. When
this luxury hotel opened in 1875, it was staffed by a full contingent of trained black employees, many with previous experi-

ence in Chicago, in service and culinary categories. In the 1880s black workers at the Palace were sharply reduced, and by the first decade of the twentieth century black workers had been completely replaced by whites.[8] Blacks planning migration to California were often urged to avoid San Francisco and to go instead to Los Angeles, which was considered a "good town for colored folks."

Job discrimination in San Francisco drove Jamaica-born J. Alexander Somerville to southern California. Finding employment in Redlands, he saved enough money to enter dental school and graduate from the University of Southern California as the first black dentist in the state. This was at the turn of the century, but Somerville was not allowed to forget his color. In his autobiography he noted that the press did not call him a Negro or a colored man when he graduated with highest honors, but referred to him as a "West Indian." He also recalled that when he sought to open an office, landlords refused to rent to him. He finally found office space in Los Angeles at Fourth and Broadway.[9]

Discrimination and racist union pressures in San Francisco caused blacks to move across the bay to Oakland and to precipitate the sharp growth of the black community in Alameda County. By 1900 Oakland's black population had grown to over a thousand, most of this increase occurring in a decade when the state's total black population experienced no growth. During that same decade Los Angeles County's black population grew from 1,817 in 1890 to 2,481 in 1900. While the greater growth of the black population would continue to be in the southern part of the state, Oakland was the one city in northern California that showed a significant, comparable growth. One reason was the rise of white unionism in San Francisco in the twentieth century.

Some of the reasons for the shifting black population can be found in national events. The years between 1890 and 1910 were bitter ones in the South, where most of the American black population still lived. The collapse of Radical Reconstruction in the late 1870s turned into full-scale disfranchisement. Racial discrimination became the daily experience of blacks, sometimes accompanied by terror, beatings, and lynchings. Those who had the means and courage to escape found only limited economic and educational opportunities elsewhere. But they were the vanguard of freedom which produced the trickle of Afro-Americans to the northern and western states.

The small growth of the black population in California until the twentieth century will require further study. What migration there was apparently came from all regions of the country. Like the gold-rush generation of blacks, the newcomers were especially energetic and daring in undertaking the long migration to the West.

A small selection of middle-class black homes in Oakland during World War I.

CHAPTER THREE

New Black Pride and Pressure Groups

THE LAST DECADE of the nineteenth century and the first of the twentieth were years of new organizational stirrings in the Afro-American world. In time they would become noticeable all over the United States and most evident in the small black middle class which wanted to be part of the volatile and ever-expanding free enterprise system of the white world. Evident, too, was activization of the civil rights struggles of an earlier era as blacks sought to reinterpret their place in society and arm what seemed to be a lost initiative. At the same time this 1890–1910 period witnessed the domestic curtailment of the civil rights of blacks in the southern states.

The keen concern for civil rights gave birth to the Afro-American Leagues. Emerging first in the northeastern states, they then spread so rapidly in California that there were enough League clubs for San Francisco to host a statewide convention in 1895. Over a hundred delegates attended, and a majority of them came from northern California counties. What was striking, however, was the large number of delegates from Los Angeles and other southland counties. A generation earlier this kind of gathering of blacks would have attracted only a handful of southern Californians. A symbolic note to this convention was the presence of some elderly delegates, men who had been prominent in black civil rights work since the gold rush. Their presence dramatized a generational transition.

The announcement for this statewide convention reflected the concerns of the California black middle class. Political, economic, and racial unity were the main themes. According to the call circulated to black communities:

> If there were a healthier desire on the part of Afro-Americans of this state to embark in business enterprises instead of the desire that at present prevails among the members of the race to be employed in menial positions, it would be but a very short time before all kinds of business enterprises controlled by colored men and women would dot many streets in the great commercial cities in the State of California.[1]

The call elaborated on this theme, suggesting areas of economic cooperation and pooling of resources for the purpose of launching businesses. Success in these endeavors would result in employment for young blacks who might otherwise not use their skills. A labor crisis was already present as the depression of the 1890s deepened, and many worried about its effects upon the nation.

The opening day of the convention got off to an impressive start with a speech of welcome by Adolph Sutro, the influential and liberal mayor of San Francisco, who had the distinction of being the only elected Populist mayor of a major city on the West Coast. His opening remarks dwelt upon the honorable history of the colored race and the challenges of the future. The stimulation of his presence and message helped the delegates settle down to business.

For three days the delegates listened to orators who covered a wide range of topics. Their speeches evoked memories of past struggles and rang with repeated calls for Afro-American unity. Black women addressed issues which reflected their growing importance in black affairs. Among their topics were "Women's Influence in Politics," "Character, Not Wealth Nor Color, the True Standard," and "The Power Woman Could Wield if She *Would.*"[2] Significantly, during the same month of the San Francisco convention, black women in the eastern states were organizing the first national black women's club movement. Boston was the setting for the birth of the National Federation of Afro-American Women, and Margaret Murray Washington, wife of Booker T., was its first president. Within a few months, affiliates formed in California. A year later the organization changed its name to the National Association of Colored Women.[3]

As the convention proceeded to discuss specific black issues, the delegates' bias for the Republican party became more and more evident when they attributed the deepening depression to the policies of Grover Cleveland's administration. In addition, they went on record against Negro colonization in other countries, supported the founding of a home for the "colored" aged in California, and favored plans for a Negro exhibition of crafts to be shown in Atlanta, Georgia, where an exposition would take place in the fall of 1895. (At this exposition Booker T. Washington would achieve national fame.) The delegates concluded their four days of deliberation with a variety of commitments to Afro-Americans, wherever they lived, but not without a flurry of internal dissension. It is not clear whether the issues resulted from clashes of principle or personality, but one group of delegates left the convention and formed another organization that within a few weeks called itself the Colored Citizens Alliance. It claimed to have primarily economic purposes and therefore not to be in conflict with the Afro-American League, which the Alliance claimed was essentially political.

During the national elections of 1896, the Afro-American League's fidelity to the Republican party was shaken. The presidential nominating convention took place in St. Louis, where Negro delegates suffered racist treatment by the host hotel and restaurants. California's black Republicans protested and even hinted at bolting the party if black delegates were not treated better. This flap had a special local flavor because Michael de Young, publisher of the *San Francisco Chronicle,* a Republican newspaper, enraged California blacks by stating that he did not believe the Republican national convention had any obligation to help black delegates in St. Louis obtain adequate housing. As a direct result, an effort to organize blacks into a William McKinley for President club failed.[4] The impact, however, was relatively slight.

The ever-shaky relationship between blacks and Republicans never reached the point of a serious break. As the twentieth century opened, the Afro-American Leagues remained Republican during election years and pressed for more civil rights at all times. The Democratic party's continued attachment to nineteenth-century racial attitudes was anathema to American blacks. In the 1900 election the McKinley-Roosevelt clubs among the blacks worked successfully for a Republican victory, and the President won by a good margin. When he was assassinated in 1901 and the Vice President, Theodore Roosevelt, became President, blacks readily accepted him. But they became most enthusiastic weeks later when the new President invited Booker T. Washington to dine with him at the White House. Washington at that time was the president of the all-black college at Tuskegee, Alabama, and a well-known speaker. His lectures to blacks directing them to spend their energies on developing vocational skills and to lay aside for a time civil rights and political activities had a special appeal to conservatives whether black or white.

Washington took an interest in the Afro-American Leagues, and his type of leadership gained influence in the movement. The leagues changed their name to Afro-American Councils about 1907 and softened their civil rights demands. Washington's racially conservative rhetoric and wide interest in white wealth made him world famous. His fame reached California as the century turned. The *San Francisco Examiner* in 1896 quoted a Yolo County newspaper thus: "Booker T. Washington would be a good man for the Cabinet."

But Washington made his greatest impact on California in 1903. For two weeks in January he toured the state and spoke about the needs of Tuskegee Institute, which was hard pressed for funds. He made money-raising speeches in San Diego, Los Angeles, Sacramento, and San Francisco as well as in other smaller towns along the way. He spoke to teachers' groups, churches, white women's clubs, and college faculties and students. The white churches were Congregational, Methodist, and Unitarian. He spoke to groups black and white and most often separately. On only one occasion, as far as it is known, was there any difficulty, and that was in San Francisco, where a white women's club sponsored one of his addresses and an Oakland black women's club thought it had a large block of tickets for the event. When the white women's club belatedly discovered that the Oakland group was black, the allotment of tickets was drastically reduced. A flurry of angry correspondence ensued, but the decision of the white women's club remained unchanged. This event, which took place in Mechanic's Pavilion where Mayor Eugene Schmitz introduced Washington to 11,000 people, was described by the *San Francisco Bulletin* as having many "colored" persons "scattered through the audience." This largely white audience gave Washington a tumultuous reception.

The press reports of Washington's visit were also laudatory and, in spite of his well-known ability to avoid civil rights issues, blacks throughout the state were proud of him. The spectacle of whites applauding a black man was intoxicating to California blacks. Even more impressive were the thousands of dollars raised by Washington for Tuskegee Institute. At the University of California, Berkeley, a large audience at a morning meeting gave him over a thousand dollars, and while he was the luncheon guest of Phoebe Apperson Hearst, she presented him with a check for five hundred dollars. Black pride was probably the most significant consequence of his California tour. The visit surely must have given a spur to Washington's other favorite organization — the National Negro Businessmen's League. [5]

When he founded the League in 1900, it reflected his philosophy of total acceptance of the free enterprise system. Through hard work and frugality, he believed, blacks could enter this system as businessmen and entrepreneurs. In California, the earliest League groups of middle-class blacks appeared in Los Angeles, San Francisco, and Oakland where they undoubtedly absorbed some of the membership and energy of the older Afro-American Councils. Probably the first meeting in California occurred in 1903 at the home of Robert C. Owens, a successful black property owner and realtor, who hosted an impressive dinner for Washington and a group of "leading colored people." Owens was probably the most distinguished member of the small black middle class of Los Angeles. He was the third generation of Owenses, who had come to California during the gold rush and intermarried with the Biddy Mason family. Owens appeared to be a favorite of Washington and was on the program of the 1907 convention of the National Negro Businessmen's League. His remarks were typical of speeches made by other delegates and carried the same theme as other remarks published by the League. They were "Horatio Alger stories" and were intended to encourage the black listener and reader to feel that he too could succeed by working hard, investing his earnings, and using his native talents.

In California, the Negro Businessmen's League had a limited existence. Its aspirations were restricted by the small size and weakness of the black middle class, which suffered from economic as well as racial discrimination. These barriers prevented blacks from using economic escalators that would give them the mobility required for significant accumulation of capital. This situation was true as well for blacks elsewhere, but the major strengths of black businessmen, as minimal as they were, were usually found in the southern states. The national conventions of the Negro Businessmen's League always showed a preponderance of southern state delegates.

The black sociologist E. Franklin Frazier wrote in his landmark study *Black Bourgeoisie* that "the National Negro Businessmen's League is based on a myth" because its convention reports presented a false image of success. Black businessmen, he claimed, not only could never command the financial resources for real success but also lacked the experience needed to achieve it. Their best hope, he believed, lay in persuading Negro buyers to patronize black businesses on the grounds of racial solidarity. Even so, they would have only limited success, for white businesses usually charged less. The League claimed that if Afro-Americans were to "buy black," then Negro employment would increase. Frazier pointed to the fragility of this argument by noting the growing number of blacks in the service and sales areas of major white corporations. He was writing in the 1950s, and today, in the 1980s with the existence of even greater black markets for white corporations, this is even more true. While the black middle class is larger today, the number of unskilled young black unemployed still remains enormous.[6]

In the first decade of California's twentieth century Booker T. Washington had a great influence in California. Organized blacks, largely of the middle class, liked him and his ideas. Other blacks at the bottom of the economic ladder knew his ideas, but his influence among them is uncertain. His first trip to California in 1903 likely inspired the founding of a significant black civic group, the Los Angeles Forum. Its leaders were a cross section of middle-class blacks concerned about the image

A gathering of Afro-American motorcar owners in Los Angeles circa 1913. A prominent guest was W. E. B. Du Bois, standing fourth from the left.

of their race and devoted to the moral and economic uplift of their community with special attention to newly arrived blacks. A decade after the founding of the Forum, they referred to Washington as "the greatest benefactor" of his race. While varying little from this basic view, the Forum successfully maintained itself for several decades as the main platform for all points of view shared by black Angelenos. Thus the Forum not only attempted to bring together many groups of blacks, but also to represent the ideological currents in the black community.[7]

Although the visit of Booker T. Washington to California had a positive impact on black leaders, not long after he left a new ideology was put forth by William E. B. Du Bois. He arrived in Los Angeles in 1913, ten years after Washington's visit, as the leading black representative of the four-year-old National Association for the Advancement of Colored People. This organization reflected the views of those blacks who accused Washington of placing civil rights at the bottom of black priorities. Joining with Du Bois, who held a Harvard University doctorate, they worked to change the emphasis.

As the picture of Du Bois in Los Angeles suggests, his followers were not devoid of middle-class attributes, but their sense of self-esteem demanded more than material accumulation. This is reflected in remarks made by Du Bois during his visit to California:

> Los Angeles is not Paradise, much as the sight of its lilies and roses might lead one at first to believe. The color line is there sharply drawn. Women have had difficulty in having gloves and shoes fitted at the stores, the hotels do not welcome colored people, the restaurants are not for all that hunger. . . . The new blood of California . . . has captured Los Angeles, but is just penetrating Oakland and San Francisco. In these latter cities the older easier-going colored man, born free . . . , still holds sway and looks with suspicion upon the Southern and Eastern newcomer. Then, too, the white trades unions have held the Negro out and down, so that here one finds a less hopeful, pushing attitude.[8]

In the decade of Du Bois's visit World War I broke out, bringing to California many young and energetic blacks seeking employment. Some were writers, attracted especially by the vigor of black journalism in southern California. The *Negro Year Book* for 1916–1917 reported nine black newspapers for the state—five of them in Los Angeles and one in Bakersfield. Two were published in Oakland, reflecting the growing importance of that community in contrast to San Francisco, where there was evidently no longer a black local paper. The only other black newspaper was published in Sacramento.

In the years following Du Bois's visit, the National Association for the Advancement of Colored People (NAACP) and the Urban League—two long-lived national black organizations—chartered western branches. The new leaders of these societies had received training in church and fraternal organizations, which had been long a part of California black community life. Among the denominations preeminent in the earlier years were the African Methodist Episcopal churches, but, as time went by, the black Baptist churches shared in this responsibility. In fact, as the migrations from the South swelled the population, the Baptists became the largest of the black denominations. They shared importance, however, in enriching the life of middle-class black Californians and providing leadership experience with the black Masonic lodges which had vitalized the social life of eastern Afro-Americans for decades.

Even before the emergence of the NAACP in California, independent black women's groups actively promoted the improvement of black communities. As early as 1899 women in Oakland organized the first black women's group under the name of the Cosmos Club. They offered a platform for distinguished eastern black speakers visiting the state. Shortly after its formation the Cosmos Club sponsored a talk by Fannie Jackson Coppin, an important black educator from Philadelphia. Members were so impressed that they changed the group's name to the Fannie Jackson Coppin Club, and as black women's organizations proliferated in the years that followed, groups named after this educator appeared throughout the state. Others bore the names of such famous black women as Sojourner Truth and Phillis Wheatley. Before World War I these clubs were involved in welfare work, anticipating the community services of the Urban League. By 1906 they had come together to form a State Federation of Colored Women's Clubs which had twenty-nine branches by 1911. Seventeen of them were in southern Cali-

fornia, with eight in Los Angeles. They were primarily concerned wtih the care of the aged and children, homemaking,
and moral uplift, including an educational campaign against
alcohol.

But most blacks soon turned to issues of civil rights which
became the preoccupation of the NAACP, which was founded in
1909. This eastern organization brought together a few black
and white liberals who were justly outraged at the racism so
evident in the nation. They also reflected the concerns of the
Progressive Era of reform before World War I. The early years
were an uphill struggle under the leadership of W. E. B. Du
Bois, whose 1913 visit to California coincided with the establishment of the state's first NAACP chapter in Los Angeles. Two
years later there was another chapter in northern California with
its strongest base in Oakland. By 1916 these two chapters
constituted the largest membership in the state, with 52 members in Los Angeles and an additional 150 in Northern California. Within a few years chapters were formed in Bakersfield,
Sacramento, Pasadena, and in even smaller black communities
as well. What made the NAACP in California especially visible
was an event in the white world of the movie industry.

In 1915 David Wark Griffith completed his artistically breath-
taking and ideologically destructive film *Birth of a Nation,* based
on Thomas Dixon's novel *The Clansman.* This film, with its
path-breaking innovations, presented nearly three hours of dis-
torted Civil War and Reconstruction history which made blacks
into one-dimensional childlike fools, incompetents, brutes, or
lechers. In San Francisco and Los Angeles the NAACP fought to
have the film either suppressed or censored. In San Francisco
some offensive footage was actually cut, but not in Los Angeles,
where the *California Eagle,* one of the earliest twentieth-century
black newspapers, campaigned unsuccessfully for editing.[9]

The film, nonetheless, raised in a negative way the issue
of black self-respect and dignity which helped lead to the
foundation of the Universal Negro Improvement Association,
organized by a flamboyant and colorful Jamaican black, Marcus
Garvey. The ingredients of black nationalism and black self-
sufficiency in Garvey's philosophy came easily to the leaders of
the Forum who, prior to the western advent of the UNIA,
already shared these ideas. Forum founder John Wesley Coleman

as early as 1920 had organized in Los Angeles a "National Convention of Peoples of African Descent." The Forum movement was soon overshadowed, however, by Garveyism. Also significant were the black self-sufficiency elements in Booker T. Washington's ideas which were accepted by Garvey. Though many Forum leaders entered easily into the Garvey movement, they made sure that the Forum itself continued to be an umbrella organization in Los Angeles that could share leadership with the NAACP.

While the UNIA attained its greatest strength in numbers and had a local chapter by 1921 in Los Angeles, the Garvey movement in fact had even earlier organized locals in San Francisco and San Diego. The appeal rested on its pride in blackness, its evocation of African glory, and its call for black economic self-sufficiency. Occasionally, it even made much of the superiority of full blackness and showed contempt for lighter black skins. The theme had its appeal among poorer Afro-Americans, who were also attracted by the full range of extravagant titles and colorful uniforms. This style of organization stood in considerable contrast to the professional and intellectual habits of the legalistic-minded NAACP. In the eastern states the hostility between the NAACP and the UNIA at times reached considerable intensity.

Yet Emory Tolbert, the historian for the UNIA in California, found that such heights of antagonism were not reached in Los Angeles or anywhere else in California. Perhaps this harmony was the result of overlapping membership. The umbrella effect of the Los Angeles Forum might have also contributed to an environment of greater tolerance among blacks in that city. By 1926 the UNIA had sixteen divisions or chapters in California.

Conflict did emerge, however, not between the NAACP and the UNIA, but rather within the UNIA itself. Garvey's dominance over the UNIA was more appearance than reality, and some of the sharpest internal conflict had its source in California. UNIA leadership there was unhappy with the careless bookkeeping of the national organization and said so openly. Furthermore, their orientation was more toward hardheaded economic accomplishment and much less toward the fanfare of spiritual excitement in Pan-Africanism. By the end of the decade and with the onset of the Great Depression, the UNIA faded away, while the NAACP survived. This kind of black nationalism with its eyes turned to Africa would surface again in the 1960s in new and more strident forms.

For the post–World War I years, life in California was attractive to many blacks. Frenzied real-estate competition reduced prices and enticed some blacks of modest income to become homeowners. This benefit of the market was particularly true in Los Angeles and Oakland, where the number of black homeowners was proudly reported from time to time in the national black press and where great numbers of blacks held jobs on the lower rungs of the civil service. In 1917, Oakland blacks, then estimated to number about five thousand, proudly published a *Colored Directory* with scores of pictures of their homes and churches. The introduction noted that the directory had grown from 76 pages in 1915 to 140 in 1917 and further observed that "the colored man's property in Northern California certainly is more conspicuous today than ever before and clearly indicates possibilities that defy the most active human imagination to fully comprehend his final development." [10]

The directory received the compliments of Booker T. Washington and other influential black readers. Further evidence of the euphoria that possessed some Oakland blacks can be seen in the 1915 poem reproduced in the directory: "I Love You, California."

In Los Angeles blacks broke into the civil service and, minimal as the jobs were, they opened up the possibility of many more jobs in the future. Los Angeles had hired blacks as policemen as early as the late 1880s when there were two on the force. While civil service entry for blacks was usually at the lowest levels, their salaries were higher than the wages paid in the South and elsewhere in the Southwest. For blacks in these regions, living in southern California seemed attractive, the more so because the prospects for factory employment were also present. To a significant extent this was a result of Los Angeles being largely a nonunion town. In 1926 Charles S. Johnson, a black sociologist at Fisk University, surveyed black employment in Los Angeles industry and found that out of 456 plants at least 50 hired blacks at various levels of skills and income. He even observed a few black foremen supervising Mexican and Anglo workers. Johnson's study revealed that racial taboos were

---

SOUVENIR

Concert Extraordinary
OAKLAND, CAL., 1915

PROF. R. G JACKSON

I LOVE YOU, CALIFORNIA
F. B. SILVERWOOD

I love you, California; you're the greatest state of all'
I love you in the winter, summer, spring, and in the
    fall,
I love your fertile valleys; your dear mountains I adore
I love your grand old ocean, and I love your rugged
    shore.

CHORUS—*William Nauns Ricks*

You are welcome to dear California,
Professor Jackson, for your fame;
From the East to the West you are known as the best
That from old Kansas ever came.
There the noble John Brown sought our freedom,
Here we glory in his name.
So we welcome you more to the State we adore
To our dear old California.

I love your old gray Missions, love your vineyards
    stretching far;
I love you California, with your Golden Gate ajar;
I love your purple sunsets, love your skies of azure
    blue,
I love you, California, I just can't help loving you.

---

a job boon for some blacks in a department store. In this case
management replaced white male "attendants" and elevator men
with blacks in order to stop time-wasting flirtation and con-
versation between white male and female employees. [11]

The image of California, at least of southern California, as an attractive place for blacks to live was undoubtedly strengthened in 1928 when the first western convention of the NAACP took place in Los Angeles. Well supported by the local NAACP chapters, the convention received great preparation and opened with much fanfare. State and local officials gave the event further stature by their presence and their welcoming speeches.

The convention had an additional unique ingredient. It took place in a just-completed, elegant hotel in a good neighborhood. The attractive establishment, which catered to both races, was named the Somerville after its owner, the West Indian–born black who had become a successful dentist in Los Angeles. The hotel was on Forty-first and Central, not far from the Coliseum, and when it hosted the 1928 NAACP convention, it accommodated such well-known people of the white and black worlds as Lincoln Steffens, W. E. B. Du Bois, Arthur Spingarn, and James Weldon Johnson. Somerville lost the hotel a year or two later in the crash and depression, and the new owners renamed the establishment in honor of the famous black poet Paul Laurence Dunbar. [12]

While blacks continued to migrate to California, once arrived they found the state something less than an interracial paradise. In the large cities there were hotels that would not receive them, restaurants that would not serve them, and innumerable public places, such as swimming pools and parks, that would not admit them. Even black and white nurses attending white patients in hospitals were required to eat in separate dining rooms. But the most glaring handicap of the 1920s was the use of real-estate covenants to prevent the settlement of blacks into new areas. Overcrowding and other economic factors deteriorated the quality of life and gradually black residential areas turned into slums. The NAACP waged legal struggles to prevent discrimination and won a few victories.

In the rural areas of the state the segregation of blacks was even more intense. The degree of racial prejudice among rural Californians, many of them originally from the South and poorly educated, was more pronounced than in the urban areas. Many of the blacks were pickers of fruit and cotton, living often in dire poverty and having few roots in the farming communities. Their clothes reflected fashions of an earlier day (usually hand-me-downs), and their homes were miserable. Their children were at the bottom of the classes, poorly prepared because the family moved frequently during the school year and with the seasons for the ripening crops. Such misery suggested desperate measures.

At the turn of the century Afro-Americans attempted to create self-sufficient black-controlled, all-black towns. Attempts had been made in Kansas and Oklahoma with varying degrees of success. In California a former army chaplain, Colonel Allen Allensworth, was the town organizer. Born a slave, he had escaped to freedom before the Civil War and, after some years, had entered the ministry. He became a chaplain in the 24th Infantry of "buffalo soldiers" fame. During the Spanish-American War he was still in this capacity and at the end of that conflict he had retired with the rank of lieutenant colonel. Settling in California, Allensworth hoped to create in the state an all-black community that would be self-sufficient, a model of accomplishment, and a place where black people could live with dignity and provide evidence of their ability to achieve.

Allensworth chose an isolated site in Tulare County for his dream city, and by 1910 the first of several hundred settlers had arrived. For nearly a decade the town of Allensworth struggled to survive as a viable community, but too many problems arose to challenge its future. The shortage of water was a chronic difficulty in this parched country, and rail transportation was not readily available. Ironically, an additional obstacle to the development of the town came from the blacks in Los Angeles who favored integration and not separation. An Allensworth-supported proposal for an all-black state industrial school within the confines of the town had all the look of Jim Crow to the urbanized blacks of Los Angeles, a community about to give birth to its first NAACP chapter. They fought successfully against the industrial school idea. Failing to achieve economic vitality, the town's small black population dwindled and the effort was given up. In the 1980s Allensworth may achieve a new importance as a monument, since it has been declared a state historical site and funds are being raised to restore it. [13]

Of considerable significance was the entry of California blacks into politics. In 1919 the first black state legislator arrived in Sacramento. He was Ohio-born Republican Frederick M. Rob-

Somerville Hotel in 1928, when this Los Angeles black-owned hotel was the site for the first NAACP national convention in the West. (*Photo by Miriam Mathews*)

erts, a learned man with a background in teaching and journalism. He edited and published *New Age,* a Los Angeles black newspaper. Assemblyman Roberts continued to represent his Los Angeles district until 1934. In these years professional black politicians were still attached to the party of Lincoln. With the exception of some elements of progressivism in the Democratic party of New York, there was still little to attract blacks to the Democratic party nationally. The southern and racist wing of the party still dominated it and Congress in so many ways that most blacks in the United States saw only the rope of the lynch mob and the cloak of the Ku Klux Klan in the Democratic party. Not until the presidency of Franklin Delano Roosevelt did that feeling change. But with the arrival of Frederick Roberts on the scene, there was the first evidence that blacks in California were preparing to shape western history and not be passively shaped by it. While Roberts's public career needs to be studied, he clearly supported social measures and often tried successfully to prevent racist materials from being used in the California schools.[14] Prejudice is often difficult to detect, however, and harder to eliminate. But Roberts labored to gain justice for blacks.

If significant political strength for blacks in the state was a long way off, economic opportunity also continued to lag in the 1910s and 1920s. Blacks held only the barest grip on industrial employment in the state, and in the wide range of service and menial employment where blacks were numerous, these years introduced a new competition. Many southern European, Mexican, and Filipino immigrants were arriving in California and seeking jobs on the lower rungs of the economic ladder. Since the new arrivals were accustomed to standards of living even much lower than those of black Americans, they were in demand by employers of unskilled labor. Yet at the same time blacks continued to come to California and intensified the growing congestion. Increasingly, the new blacks of the 1920s left the rural southwestern states and brought with them the usual unfamiliarity with urban living that marked all migrants from the farm to the city. Rural American white migrants and European immigrants had organizations like the YMCA and YWCA to guide them, and the famed settlement houses to prepare them for city life, but there were no similar provisions for American blacks. Into this void entered the Urban League. Even before World War I it was at work in the major urban centers of the East. By the 1920s it had recognized a need for social service and job-seeking functions in California. Organizers were sent west and efforts were made in the Bay Area as well as in Los Angeles to found chapters of the Urban League. By the end of the 1920s one was functioning well in Los Angeles where the ghettoization of the black community had become ever more vivid.

One cannot leave the decade of the 1920s without considering the enormous growth of the motion picture industry in Hollywood and its impact on blacks. Historians of the film industry cite 1915 as the year in which California film making developed into a serious art form. In that year, as already noted, the remarkable but intensely antiblack *Birth of a Nation* was presented to the public by its brilliant southern-born director-producer, David Wark Griffith. It was produced in southern California where blacks were employed to play in mob scenes and to portray menials. Leading black roles were played by whites in blackface.

As described earlier, many blacks joined with the NAACP in picketing and protesting this film in California as well as in the rest of the country. Other blacks went into the movie-making business to change the image of Afro-Americans as depicted in *Birth of a Nation.* Most of these efforts took place in the East, but one attempt by blacks, considered by theater historians as the most valiant and sophisticated, was filmed in Los Angeles by the brothers George and Noble Johnson. The latter was a frequent character player in Universal Pictures who used his spare time to launch the Lincoln Company. George, a full-time postal employee in Omaha, Nebraska, almost half a continent away, assisted his brother in preparing bookings for their productions.

The Johnson brothers were determined to avoid white investors because many of them were either unreliable or used their influence to reintroduce Negro stereotypes to the stories. The Johnsons were committed to presenting black life free of stereotypes. They felt that the large urban black communities that emerged from coast to coast during the aftermath of the Civil War and intense decades of industrialization would provide a rewarding market for black film makers. By the 1920s thousands of blacks were already living in New York's Harlem, Chicago's South Side, and Los Angeles's Watts, not to mention the urban centers in the southern states.

Between 1915 and 1921, under great and constant financial strain, the Johnson brothers produced a variety of films, including *The Realization of a Negro's Ambition, The Trooper of Troop K, A Man's Duty,* and *By Right of Birth.* These movies portrayed the values of the work ethic and the triumph of virtue. *By Right of Birth,* the last film that the Lincoln Company produced, treated the delicate subject of "passing" — the practice of some very light-skinned Negroes casting off their ethnic identity in the white world. This last film barely broke even financially in spite of an intensive promotional campaign that exhausted the meager financial resources of the Johnson brothers. They also employed members of the affluent black community of Los

Angeles in bit parts (among them the prominent Booker T. Washington, Jr., a Los Angeles realtor) and ten of the prettiest black women in Los Angeles to sell tickets. In writing of this event, film historian Thomas Cripps said, "There simply was not enough spending money in black Los Angeles to sustain more than a split week, even after a strenuous promotional effort."

In 1921 the Lincoln Motion Picture Company, facing eventual bankruptcy, gave up. The financial problems were more than it could handle. Support from the black community was too limited, and black film producers elsewhere in the country were also looking for money, thus fragmenting the potential financial resources of Afro-Americans. While there were wealthy blacks in the United States, they were too few in number to provide the necessary assistance. After the company was liquidated, Noble Johnson returned to the white film world to play black and Indian character roles.[15]

In those films blacks continued through the 1920s and into the 1930s to play buffoons, musicians, and menials. Racial stereotypes prevailed. Blindness by white producers in this matter is highlighted by a list of "Don'ts and Be Carefuls" adopted in 1927 by the California Association of the Motion Picture Producers and Distributors of America, Inc. Among the thirty-six "Don'ts" were "miscegenation (sexual relationships between white and black races)" and "willful offense to any nation, race or creed." Certainly, on the second point producers were violating their own code wittingly or unwittingly.

However, in 1940 an event occurred in Hollywood that signaled a shift in attitude. The tremendous impact of *Gone With the Wind* burst on the movie world. Its star-studded cast, including Clark Gable and Vivien Leigh, guaranteed box-office success. The inclusion of unpleasant black stereotypes, however, recalled the racism of earlier films, but before a year had passed much of the anger was blunted by an unusual development. The leading black female character in *Gone With the Wind,* Hattie McDaniel, playing a strong character as a slave housekeeper, won an "Oscar" for her role. She was the first black in the film industry to win the coveted prize. From this point on, blacks appeared more frequently in film productions though still in parts with limited dimensions.

World War II and the revulsion against Hitler's racist theories contributed to the changing mood in Hollywood. The industry registered a growing antifascist temper, and blacks soon were seen in films of social commentary. Directors approached discrimination and race relations a bit more directly. Scripts were written with more roles for blacks. This development accompanied a sharp rise in the employment of blacks as actors in the industry. The trend came to an abrupt end during the immediate postwar years as a consequence of the Cold War and the Red-hunt of the Joseph McCarthy era that accompanied it. Black employment in films was the innocent victim of the witch hunt in Hollywood conducted by the House Committee on Un-American Activities. The jailings and blacklistings that resulted drove from Hollywood many writers who produced the kinds of scripts that gave employment to black actors. Such scripts, because they dealt with social problems, were perceived as subversive by the House committee. For about a decade blacks found little employment in the film industry in roles other than as entertainers and menials. In 1963 a reversal came with the Oscar-winning performance of Sidney Poitier in *Lilies of the Field.* From then on black actors of both sexes experienced a rise in the number of quality roles.

In nonacting professions in Hollywood blacks were seldom in evidence. The motion picture industry's hiring practices were part of the explanation, but the preferences of blacks played a part as well. An article in *Crisis,* the NAACP magazine, reported in February 1946 that "on the whole Negroes have not concerned themselves . . . with the less glamorous phases of moviemaking and have concentrated specifically on acting." [16] In the more than thirty years since that report, the number of nonacting black professionals in film making has increased sharply as a result of job opportunities in television and the movies. The film-making departments of the colleges and universities in California can attest to the rise in interest by black students in this glamorous occupation.

Afro-Americans entered the American movie era playing roles that were demeaning stereotypes. They were invisible as total human beings. As the industry and its cultural environment matured unevenly, blacks began to appear occasionally as whole persons. The Stepin Fetchits were gradually replaced by the

Sidney Poitiers. And in the 1960s and 1970s black movie makers Gordon Parks and Melvin Van Peebles moved closer to center stage with their work. Blacks today are totally visible and in a variety of dimensions in cinema and television, though the number of job opportunities remains a sore point. Moreover, black critics of the movie industry are troubled by the very profitable "Super Fly" and "Beverly Hills Cop" images. Undoubtedly, how blacks appear on film will continue to be a subject of controversy, but the indications are that the American public, white and black, will make the decisions through preferences at the ticket cage.

CHAPTER FOUR

Depression and War

T HE GREAT DEPRESSION of the 1930s paradoxically stimu-
lated one of the largest migrations of southern blacks to
California. Only slightly fewer blacks came than had migrated
in the prosperous 1920s. Of course, this era was also marked by
a surprisingly large migration to the West of whites from Oklahoma, Kansas, and Texas who wanted to escape the dust storms
and the depression.

A glance at the *California Eagle,* the major Negro newspaper
in Los Angeles during the depression, makes the migration of
blacks during these years seem astonishing. Its pages were full
of stories about police brutality, job discrimination, and segregation. An historian of the period who interviewed some of the
newcomers found that letters from friends and relatives were
the major reasons the migrants had set out for Los Angeles.[1]
They evidently had not seen copies of the *California Eagle* before
their arrival.

Even with this unusual migration of blacks, the overall general migration westward was so enormous that in 1940 blacks
still were barely two percent of the total California population.
Though the entire state received additions to its population,
the larger part went to the southern cities of the state. Over
24,000 blacks settled in Los Angeles, and of the four cities
other than Los Angeles that got more than a thousand new
black residents in this decade, San Diego led the way, followed
by Fresno, San Francisco, and Berkeley.[2]

The attraction that southern California had for blacks in this hungry decade was a blend of fact and expectation. The wave of unemployment that struck the country hit California later than elsewhere, but when it swept over the state in the early 1930s, blacks suffered the highest unemployment rate of any group in Los Angeles. In 1931 nearly 50 percent of all blacks were unemployed in the city. By 1935 above 40 percent of the black families of Los Angeles were on relief, and most of those fortunate to have jobs had the lowest-paying ones in the state. Organized labor prevented them from getting a serious foothold in industrial employment, although before World War II the state did not have much heavy industry. On the brighter side, blacks owned more homes in southern California than elsewhere in the nation and enjoyed income from low-paying jobs in Los Angeles that was higher than in the rest of the country. Furthermore, like most whites, blacks enjoyed the mild weather and accepted more easily the burden of unemployment where the sun shone regularly and where aid was available. Of great significance, too, were the beginnings of the vast national relief program that was provided by the Franklin D. Roosevelt administration.

In the election of 1932 hard times swept Roosevelt into power as President. The Democratic party victory reflected his crisp leadership as governor of New York as well as the dire economic conditions in the country. The incumbent Republican President, Herbert C. Hoover, appeared to be incapable of coping effectively or dramatically with the problems of the depression. Roosevelt's administration moved rapidly to enact programs which provided help for over 15 million unemployed nationally and the million and a quarter unemployed locally (about 20 percent of the state's population). Of course, most blacks in California were eligible for the benefits of these programs, and many needed immediate help. Some found jobs in the best-known and most reviled New Deal program, the Works Progress Administration (WPA), which sponsored about 85 percent of the public construction projects in the United States.

During the years of the WPA's operation (1935–1941), more than a million black Americans benefited from federal relief jobs. Tens of thousands of workers were California blacks, primarily in Los Angeles, San Francisco, and Oakland. Most of them did manual labor on the many WPA construction projects in the state. However, some hundreds were employed in the performing arts in the Federal Music and Theatre projects in California. Well-trained Negro musicians taught music and conducted programs in Los Angeles and Oakland. An all-black cast and chorus performed an opera in Los Angeles. In 1937 and 1938 the Federal Music and Federal Theatre projects collaborated in producing a musical play composed by the famous black choir leader Hall Johnson, with a cast of 150 Afro-Americans. It was called *Run Little Chillun* and played to large audiences in California.[3]

The depression affected almost everyone, but Roosevelt's party did much to restore confidence throughout the nation. There was need, however, for new grass-roots leadership. Ever since 1919 black Republican leader Frederick M. Roberts had represented an assembly district in Los Angeles. In 1934 he was challenged by a black Democrat, Augustus F. Hawkins, who waged a strong campaign and defeated him. Hawkins's victory signaled the California phase of the shift taking place nationally as the traditionally Republican blacks gave their allegiance to the Democratic party. Hawkins, the son of a successful Louisiana pharmacist, had come with his parents to Los Angeles in 1917 when he was ten years old. His father, disgusted with living in the South, had sought a good environment, schools, and financial opportunity for his family. In 1931 the young Hawkins received his degree in economics from UCLA and entered immediately into the real estate business. In 1934 he was swept up by the excitement and idealism of Upton Sinclair's E.P.I.C. campaign which challenged the Republican party. While Sinclair's political career as a maverick Democrat was brief and meteoric, Hawkins continued much less spectacularly as an elected official committed to liberal causes and reelected year after year.

The 1934 gubernatorial contest was unusual because of the emotion aroused in the electorate. Sinclair was an anti-Communist Socialist best known for his enormous volume of writing on social issues and the plans he intended to implement if he were elected governor. There was some black support for Sinclair, but how much is not clear. An official of the black Dining Car Cooks and Waiters Union organized Sinclair support clubs in

Los Angeles and Oakland. Other blacks offered their personal backing, but the anti-Sinclair forces were also active. They drenched the black communities with statements about Sinclair's views on organized religion. These attacks, designed to make Sinclair look like an atheist (which he was not), clearly influenced many California voters. An anti-Sinclair film clip shown throughout California falsely purported to be a newsreel interview with a black minister who said that he was voting for Sinclair's opponent, Republican Frank Merriam, because the minister wanted to "save his church." The black "minister" was a local prize fighter who also preached. While much bitterness resulted from this kind of electioneering, the vote was nonetheless surprisingly close. Fortunately for Hawkins, he was able to sidestep the hostility, and California continued to have a single black elected official. Not until 1948 would the people elect another black assemblyman, Byron Rumford of Berkeley.

The defeat of Upton Sinclair raises questions about the extent to which a radical philosophy had any appeal for blacks in California. The record suggests, for example, that Marxism had magic for a relatively small number. There were only a few black Socialists before World War I and very few in later years. A left-wing-led trade union of farm workers in the Imperial Valley called a strike early in 1930, and a black journalist noted with pride that there was not one Negro included. Of course, this also reflected how few black farm workers there were in the region. A few years later, during the Great Depression, some California blacks found the Communist party appealing because it was the only political party to defend them. Some worked for the Communist party in the National Negro Congress, which became a front organization, but this relationship was not of long duration. The slight Communist penetration of the NAACP was soon driven out by the NAACP leadership.[4] The masses of blacks in the thirties and forties, while rarely hostile to Communists, were passive to their Marxism and overwhelmingly favored democratic ideologies. A possible explanation for the indifference of the black masses to the Communists may derive from their largely rural and religious backgrounds. This indifference to radical ideologies they shared with most rural southern whites as well.

The fragmentary story of blacks in California agriculture revealed an indifference of another kind: an indifference, perhaps even hostility, to the farming life. Only a handful of blacks who had come during the gold rush turned to farming, especially on the outskirts of Marysville, Chico, and Stockton. After the Civil War, some black veterans may have received land bounties in California, but most moved into the towns where they wanted to become wage earners. Several efforts were made by whites to plant cotton in the San Joaquin Valley with black labor brought there from the former slave states. These cotton "plantations" were short-lived, largely because the blacks left this kind of work as soon as they could since it reminded them of slavery days. The anti-Chinese agitation in California in the 1880s led officials of several southern railroad lines to believe that there would shortly be a harvest labor shortage in California. Knowing that conditions for southern Negroes in those years were worsening, they organized a "colored" labor agency to bring blacks to the California fields. For reasons yet unknown, this effort failed to produce any significant westward movement of blacks. During the rest of the nineteenth century, few blacks entered California agriculture.

When the Imperial Valley opened to agriculture, blacks were recruited as laborers. Few blacks, however, answered the call, in spite of the fact that the *California Eagle,* a black-owned Los Angeles newspaper, printed ads for cotton pickers in Calexico. Actually the growers favored Mexican labor, especially because of cost and supply. In the decade following World War I, however, a sprinkling of black farmers (not farm laborers) appeared in the Imperial Valley. When Charlotta Bass and her husband, who was the editor of the *California Eagle,* visited Imperial City on a Sunday in January 1918, they found sixty black families, thirty of them active members of the local black Baptist church. Some of the blacks had started out as laborers, but by 1930 most were independent farmers. These black agriculturalists in the Imperial Valley, though small in number, came exclusively from the southern and southwestern states. In spite of their modest success, few migrants followed their footsteps into the valley.

While John Steinbeck's *Grapes of Wrath,* both as novel (1939) and film (1940), projected an image of only white immigrant poverty in California agriculture, scholarly studies of California farm labor before and after World War II mention Mexican, Japanese, and Filipino migrant workers. The surveys occasionally reveal some black workers. At one point in the 1930s there were 149 farm labor contractors who were overwhelmingly Mexicans and native whites, but fourteen of them were Negroes, suggesting some small percentage of black farm laborers.

Elsewhere, Victorville, a small town about a hundred miles northeast of Los Angeles and best known today for its dry climate, became the locale of a vast movie set for making westerns, including many of the films starring William S. Hart. It was also the area in which some Los Angeles blacks in 1914 attempted to create a community of farmers. Their effort had only limited appeal, and by the 1920s had faded, although a small black community emerged in the town of Victorville. Perhaps the attraction of bit movie parts or the opportunity for part-time work in cowboy film production proved more attractive to these blacks than farming.

Another episode in the fragmentary history of blacks in California agriculture occurred in 1945 at the conclusion of World War II. The shutting down of many war plants in the Bay Area swiftly placed thousands of blacks in the ranks of the unemployed because as the last hired, they were the first to be fired. Some of these people found work on the fruit and nut farms of the Chico area, where laborers were in short supply. The crops that harvest season of 1945 were bountiful and laborers were not available in sufficient numbers. To meet the crisis, the Chico area growers and labor agencies came together in Richmond, California, and decided to engage unemployed Richmond blacks for the harvest, since many of them had been familiar with agricultural work in their home states of the South and Southwest. Unfortunately, even before these black workers arrived, the nongrower elements in Chico feared an influx of blacks. The prejudice grew serious in spite of the fact that Chico had a small black community which had flourished there for several generations. But the newer and much more youthful group alarmed them. The local growers, whose economic needs had more leverage than the town dwellers of

Chico, succeeded in bringing in the first shipment of black workers. They were housed in a specially selected area. These strangers had to face a barrage of "white only" signs in many, if not most, of the stores and restaurants, but the experiment succeeded and was even repeated for several years. Their numbers were never as large as the growers would have desired because reports of prejudice in Chico reached Richmond and changed the minds of some blacks who had considered this work. For several years, however, hundreds of them participated in this program. Apparently growers in other parts of the Sacramento and San Joaquin valleys also participated in similar programs. How long blacks worked as migrant laborers in the Central Valley is not clear, but as late as 1957 twenty-five Negro families (with one water faucet and two showers to serve all of them) lived in shacks near Marysville while they worked to harvest a peach crop. Probably none of these people ever became part of the local communities.[5]

Among the immediate consequences of World War II were accelerated shipbuilding and aircraft production and new jobs. Advertisements in eastern and southern newspapers magnified the opportunities which were often spectacular. During 1941 migration to California rose sharply over the previous three years, and blacks were part of this influx. Again, southern California received the lion's share of these newcomers. A much larger proportion of blacks than ever before came from the South and the Southwest. They heard of the job opportunities through many channels. Most effective were the notices of job openings in the shipbuilding and aircraft industries that went out through the thousands of state employment offices in every state in the nation. This writer remembers seeing such notices in a small town in Illinois in 1942 referring to such exotic locations as Mare Island and Hunter's Point. For blacks in the South this was a great opportunity to escape the low wage scales there. Until 1942, however, defense jobs elsewhere in the nation drew many more blacks proportionally than did those in California.

Even so, until late 1942 blacks experienced much opposition on racial grounds from employers. Their indifference or discrimination, compounded by union restrictions, had held down the number of jobs available to blacks. Not until the dramatic

threat in 1941 by A. Philip Randolph, the black president of
the Sleeping Car Porters Union, of a protest march on Washington did President Roosevelt issue Executive Order 8802. This
order required defense training programs to end discrimination
and inserted a nondiscrimination clause into government defense contracts. It also set up a Committee on Fair Employment
Practices. Armed with federal authority and support, blacks
exerted pressure for the first time upon employers to open up
jobs for them in the defense industry. Employers and unions
now began to unbend. The order strengthened the hands of
those employers and unions which had hired blacks even before
this pressure. The CIO, for example, had been actively opposed
to discrimination since its founding. On the West Coast, the
most conspicuous example of such opposition to racial discrimination was in the International Longshoremen's and Warehousemen's Union (ILWU), headed by the outspoken Harry Bridges,
which wielded enormous power. Additional factors breaking
down discrimination during these war years were the enormous
growth of the aircraft industry in southern California, the expansion of the building and maintenance industry in the Bay
area, and the need of a large labor pool.[6]

These new job opportunities for blacks raised serious issues
concerning unionism. In the 1870s, the close ties among labor
organizations, the Workingmen's party, and Irish leaders had
served to keep blacks out of labor organizations. This exclusion,
in turn, had made blacks indifferent, if not hostile, to the
interests of organized labor. In 1881 a group of skilled workmen
created an association, soon known as the American Federation
of Labor (AFL), which was composed largely of craft unions that
excluded Negroes from membership. The opportunity for employment in the better-paying skilled jobs had been a way in
which white workers or their children moved into the middle
class in American life. This opportunity was denied to all blacks
and to many white workers when they were denied membership
in the AFL.

With few changes, this background reflects the conditions of
black-union relationship into the twentieth century. Because of
political changes in Los Angeles that took place between 1910
and 1911 the Central Labor Council initiated cooperative activities with black community organizations for the first time.

Harry Bridges, president of ILWU, and some of the union's full-time leaders: top row, left to right: Albert James, hiring hall dispatcher for San Francisco Longshore Local 10; Howard Bodine, Coast Labor Relations committeeman; William Chester, ILWU Northern California Regional Director, and Louis Goldblatt, International secretary-treasurer; botton row: John Walker, dispatcher for Local 10 and member of Northern California District Council; Harry Bridges, and Claude Saunders, Local 10 executive board member.

Several union representatives joined the local Afro-American League to form the Mutual Organization League. Its purpose was to bring Negro workers into the organized labor movement. They met in the recently constructed and elegant Labor Temple, which housed, in addition to the Los Angeles trade union offices, the Socialist party headquarters and the interracial Mutual Organization League. This antiracist thrust occurred at a moment in Los Angeles labor history when the local Socialist party had its greatest influence on the local labor movement. The period of Socialist influence was short-lived and so was the antiracist effort.

Until the birth in the 1930s of a new labor organization called the Congress of Industrial Organizations (CIO), blacks

were used often as strikebreakers in California as well as elsewhere in the United States. Since they were excluded from the
ranks of organized labor, blacks had little empathy with white
workers. It should be mentioned, however, that in many cases
blacks were used to break strikes unwittingly. In some cases
they were actually given the impression that they were being
offered legitimate employment.

Strikebreaking in the 1930s diminished greatly when the International Longshoremen's and Warehousemen's Union (ILWU)
opened its ranks to blacks. This practice slowly spread to other
organizations but with spectacular results for coming generations. When the impact of World War II hit the West Coast,
the aircraft and shipbuilding industries experienced the greatest boom. Working among the many thousands of employees in
these rapidly expanding industries was only a handful of blacks.
Southern California's aviation industry was a classic case. In
1941 only twelve blacks were employed in a work force of
60,000!

By 1942, as a consequence of the Executive Order 8802
issued by President Roosevelt, job opportunities appeared in
California, and black employment in defense industries rose.
The powerful craft unions and industrial employers gradually
yielded to federal pressure. At the Lockheed Vega plant in Los
Angeles, for example, the Machinists Union local, in spite of
the national union's "whites only" provisions, began admitting
blacks to membership. This local could have been suspended
from the national union, but it was not even censured. The
reason lay in the national union's fear that the federal government might censure it. Once more blacks found reason to look
to the federal government for support.

In another case the situation was the reverse of that involving
the Machinists' Union. A national union with the staggering
title of the Amalgamated Association of Street and Electric
Railway and Motor Coach Employees (an AFL affiliate) had an
antidiscrimination clause in its national charter. During the
war, Los Angeles public transportation was overcrowded and
understaffed. Demands for employing blacks to alleviate the
labor shortage came from many quarters, including the federal
government. Management and most of the white union members balked at this pressure. But federal officials insisted, and in

1943 at one location two blacks were upgraded. As an immediate consequence, eight white workers protested with a two-hour strike which had the effect of returning the black workers to their former menial and poorer-paying jobs with the local transport company. A second effort to use black labor in Los Angeles also failed. What probably broke the stubbornness of management and the balky union in 1944 was the continuing pressure by the federal government on all discriminating local transport companies across the country. An underlying element was the difficulty encountered in Los Angeles by other union workers in getting to their jobs in aircraft industries because of understaffed streetcar lines. When black workers were finally upgraded, only one white worker quit.[7]

In the San Francisco Bay area Negro workers also encountered union racism in the shipbuilding trades. The setting for the most dramatic story of wartime job discrimination in northern California was on the shoreline of the charming city of Sausalito, today a tourist mecca in Marin County. Here the Bechtel Corporation established Marinship, which built "liberty ships" and prefabricated tankers. Marinship was hiring blacks by 1942, after an earlier skirmish in Bay area shipbuilding in which an attempt to employ only white workers was defeated by local black labor leaders. However, it was the anti-black union rules of the Boilermakers' Union local, with the acquiescence of management, that created the problem.

The union's rules allowed creation of "auxiliary" locals for blacks. Members of "auxiliary" locals were required to pay full dues but had no voting power and were denied other privileges and responsibilities. Joe James, a Marinship welder, led a strike by blacks to reject "auxiliary" union status. Firings occurred, and a protracted struggle was waged from 1943 to 1945, when the war ended. With the aid of the NAACP and other blacks in the Bay area, black shipyard workers at Marinship continued to fight for full status in the Boilermakers' Union. The case moved between the newly formed Fair Employment Practices Commission and court hearings, ending with a decision in the California state supreme court that favored the Negro workers. But it came too late to benefit many of them. The end of wartime production had resulted in mass layoffs and, ironically, the end of the racist provision in the Boilermakers' Union. In 1948 all

Boilermakers' locals were integrated, but by then the controversial local had 1800 workers of whom only 150 were black. In
1944 the local membership had numbered 36,000, including
3,000 blacks in the "auxiliaries."

World War II was marked by much racial turbulence in the
armed forces as well as among urban laborers. Segregation was
still the rule in the armed forces during most of the war. In
1944 a dramatic event occurred in California at a U.S. Navy
loading station in Port Chicago, where black sailors loading
shells were caught in a terrible explosion that killed hundreds.
The men were stationed at nearby Mare Island and, not long
after the tragedy, orders were issued to start loading again. This
resulted in a mutiny in which fifty black soldiers refused to obey
the order. A court case ensued in which the local NAACP chapter, with help from its national office, fought unsuccessfully to
free the mutineers. The explosion and trial were memorialized
in the one-act play in poetic prose *Black Boat* by the prominent
white California poet Julia Cooley Altrocchi; it read in part

> Five hundred strong
> We were sent to the Port,
> Five hundred Negroes to stow and to sling,
> And death was the cargo and stark was the wrong,
> And black is the song
> That my black mouth must sing.

The play was later published in her anthology *Girls with Ocelot
and Other Poems* (Boston, 1964). Two years later, and into the
peacetime period, nearly all the men were either freed or had
their sentences reduced.

During the war and immediate postwar years the West experienced its greatest influx of people, and California received most
of this migration. The Afro-American population in California
rose from 124,306 in 1940 to 462,172 by 1950, with most of
these people in the three great centers of industry: Los Angeles,
San Francisco–Oakland, and San Diego. Most newcomers, both
white and black, came from southern and rural regions where
educational opportunities were limited and where blacks enjoyed fewer opportunities than whites. Black expectations, even
allowing for the habit of lower expectations acquired in the
southern environment, inevitably rose in this more open society. In several of the larger cities of the state, interracial councils

of civic unity and commissions on human relations were organized that gave heart to black aspirations. But these blacks and whites obviously faced problems of education which deterred plans for early upward mobility.

The war provided some significant, if short-lived, employment gains. Excluded from all but a few janitorial jobs before 1942, blacks had 7,186 jobs in Los Angeles area aircraft plants by July 1944. From a few hundred shipyard workers in 1942 they grew to 18,538, nearly 13 percent of the total, in the San Francisco–Oakland area by November 1943. Especially novel was the employment of black women in both industries, a decided breakthrough for a portion of the black labor force that as late as the 1930s was still predominantly in domestic work.

In the readjustment period after the war's end, blacks were conspicuously numerous on the unemployment compensation lines. When those funds were exhausted, the number of blacks began to rise again on the relief roles. However, not all blacks who were new to heavy industry were being laid off. A good number retained their jobs into the postwar boom, but they also faced a return of discriminatory practices. In the clerical and white-collar areas of the private sector blacks were still very few in number. The breakthrough there would have to wait until the 1960s.

Illustrative of the change in working conditions from war to peace is the story told by sociologist C. Wilson Record about the young black Willie Stokes. Record followed Stokes from his life on a cotton farm in Mississippi in 1941 through his wartime experiences as a welder in the Kaiser shipyards in Richmond, California, where he received $10 for an eight-hour day. In 1946, following the war, Stokes was laid off, and then found work in a chemical plant near Richmond at $6.40 a day for eight hours of labor. He purchased his groceries in the same stores that he had patronized during the war, but the prices were now much higher. Not only was he no longer able to live on his wages, but his situation had also worsened further since he had married and had a large family. He was forced to cash in his war bonds to make ends meet. By 1947 Willie Stokes was unemployed and surviving on unemployment compensation. This aid was of short duration and soon the family was on county relief.[8]

The near quadrupling of California's black population was not matched during the war by a comparable expansion of housing. Wartime housing was a problem for all groups in many areas of the nation, especially in such a concentrated area of defense industries as California. But the fact that ghettos were either well established by 1940 in California communities or that all the mechanisms for doing so were present (as in San Diego) made the problem of black housing particularly acute. Los Angeles blacks received a small amount of added space by occupying much of Little Tokyo after the Japanese-American evacuation. But in most areas blacks were compelled to crowd into housing little larger than in prewar periods. Some black leaders saw public housing as an answer and applauded the nomination of a black businessman (George Beavers) to direct the Los Angeles Housing Authority in 1943. Such projects as were built were segregated, located in already low-income areas (Watts, Hunter's Point), and would become in later decades centers of poverty, crime, and resentment.

For the mass of new black Californians the quality of life was also held down by the intensified real estate practice of preventing blacks from moving into new and better areas. Black residential areas which had not already become ghettos now did so, and many of these became slums as congestion worsened.

The creation of ghettos in the 1920s and 1930s and their spread by the migrations during World War II are vividly described by Lawrence de Graaf, a well-known California historian. He discovered that in the early years of the twentieth century Los Angeles Afro-Americans found homes in five separate areas not adjacent to each other. These residents were described in a local black newspaper as people who "prudently refused to segregate themselves into any locality" in order to secure not only "the best fire, water and police protection, but also the more important benefits that accrue from refined and cultural surroundings."[9]

As the number of blacks increased, white flight occurred and led to the segregation of blacks in densely populated communities. At first race restriction clauses in property sales and restrictive covenants slowed the expansion of black neighborhoods, though initially these were weakly enforced or circumvented by the collusion between black and white realtors. Commercial incentive overcame racial prejudices for a while at least. More-over, until 1919, legal rulings on residential racial restriction seesawed with some NAACP-supported individual victories for blacks. These various developments worked to the detriment of Negro housing needs. The 1920s marked a serious effort by the slowly growing black middle class to break out of its city-center areas into the ever-growing suburbs of Los Angeles. These ef-forts were a combination of searches for comfortable homes in suburbia and middle-class recreational opportunities such as seaside clubhouses. Such efforts were frustrated by white hos-tility that came to a dramatic point in Manhattan Beach. There an effort by middle-class Negroes to suburbanize was defeated by the presence of the Ku Klux Klan in the city. Not only were black newcomers denied real estate, but black residents of many years standing were also forced to move out of the city. Restric-tive covenants now multiplied and gained strength legally through a 1928 state supreme court decision that supported racist agreements which could even force black residents to sell homes they had long owned.

Over a third of the black families of Los Angeles in 1930 owned their homes, while only about 10 percent did so in Chicago, 15 percent in Detroit, and about 5½ percent in New York.[10] Also, white landlordism was less brutal in Los Angeles than in other cities because blacks tended to rent single-family homes or apartments in small building complexes far less congested than the huge tenements of eastern cities where landlond-tenant relationships were extremely impersonal. Enor-mous tenement structures do not darken the skyline of Los Angeles. It would take the mass black migration of the 1940s and 1950s into these now restricted areas of Los Angeles to give reality to the word "slum."

The now famous community of Watts provides a dramatic case study of how slums are created. Watts began as part of a Mexican ranch which was subdivided and the parcels sold to Anglos, one of whom was Julia Watts. The Pacific Electric built an interurban rail station there, and settlement developed dur-ing the years before World War I because the land was cheap. Blacks from the South created a community on the southern edge of the subdivision, and they were eventually surrounded by Mexicans and Anglos who found jobs in Los Angeles and

Long Beach. The industrialization of nearby areas during World War I brought additional blacks from the South, and the migrations of World War II intensified the congestion of the area. With the wartime building of public housing projects that were meant to be interracial but became all black, two-thirds of the Watts population became black.

The congestion that marked the growth of Watts was taking place in the other nearby but formerly separate black communities. The consequence was white flight, and the gradual fusing of the once separate ghettos into a vast black community stretching from the lower part of downtown Los Angeles to the western part of Compton. The Harbor Freeway eventually bisected this huge ghetto, and the result was a black community to the west of the freeway that is middle class and one to the east that has a clearly slum-like quality in spite of intermittent attractive, single-family dwellings. Under these demographic circumstances de facto segregation in the schools became inevitable and the cultural isolation of blacks intensified. In spite of official and unofficial reports that Watts was approaching a crisis, nothing was done until the bloody riot of 1965.

The restrictive covenant became an increasing irritant to black pride, especially to those blacks who had the income to afford comfortable homes in good neighborhoods. In the 1940s as the number of blacks in California swelled, there developed a small professional and business class whose members were among the first to feel the stinging insult of realtors who refused to sell middle-class homes to them. The refusal reflected a widespread bias of white homeowners who felt that the movement of blacks into any neighborhood brought a decline in housing prices.

White homeowners relied upon restrictive covenants to keep blacks from buying into their neighborhoods. The legality of these covenants, moreover, was endured by blacks until the end of World War II. Indeed, Asians faced similar problems. One of the first legal challenges to this practice was the "Sugar Hill" case won by black attorneys in a Los Angeles court in 1945. Two years later, concerned lawyers joined forces with the NAACP to argue the issue before the United States Supreme Court, where in 1948 the justices struck down restrictive covenants.[11] However, the decision was not strong enough to prevent discrimination in the selling and renting of homes. Nearly two decades would have to pass before that attack on housing discrimination would reach a critical level. A few legal skirmishes in middle-class neighborhoods conducted by the NAACP in the Los Angeles area were won shortly before the 1948 U.S. Supreme Court decision, but the major housing struggles were yet to come.

In the immediate postwar years battles over discrimination by public eating places and in professional organizations were fought in the Los Angeles area. The *Negro Handbook* for 1949 reported three restaurant victories where the courts awarded damages to a black complainant. Black professionals also challenged racial prejudice. In 1945, one month before the United Nations was born in San Francisco, the Los Angeles Bar Association, an all-white organization, found itself perplexed when a black attorney was put up for membership. In following tradition, the association took the stand that "the policy of the Association expressed in its constitution and in its past history is such that in the absence of a mandate from the membership to the contrary it has no other course than to deny members of the Negro race membership in the Association." Several association referenda and five years later, in 1950, the Los Angeles Bar Association gave black attorneys the right to membership by a resounding vote of 1,018 to 593.[12]

World War II also brought attention to another problem long smoldering in the black community—conflict with the local police. This issue was one that black leaders hesitated to raise, partly because it recalled long-held stereotypes of Afro-Americans as prone to crime and partly because some California cities, particularly Los Angeles, had been pioneers in the hiring of black police officers. By the 1930s, however, the hiring of blacks had not extended much beyond token numbers. Moreover, the Los Angeles Police Department was gaining a reputation as an antiradical and antilabor force with its "Red Squad." Sometimes those hostile attitudes extended to the city's minorities. In the Zoot Suit riots of 1943, which involved mostly Mexicans but a few blacks as well, the local police either looked on or aided the servicemen who assaulted these minorities. Following this shocking incident, black leaders in Los Angeles demanded reform of the police department and worked themselves to create organizations that would relieve human tensions.

At the end of the decade, when J. Alexander Somerville became the first black on the Los Angeles Police Commission, public protest over police-black relations had receded. But the basic problem persisted, however, to break out again in the 1960s. [13]

The war mobilization of the 1940s drew great numbers of blacks to California, making it one of the nation's leading centers of black population. The war also provided many blacks with their first well-paying jobs and led to the creation of new community organizations. But the war also highlighted some major issues — jobs, housing, and police relations — that would be prime targets of protest by California blacks for the next two decades.

CHAPTER FIVE

From Agitation
to Revolt

N O ADULT CALIFORNIANS in 1945, whether black or white,
had more than the faintest idea that within twenty years
racial turbulence in their state would reach unprecedented dimensions. They were not unmindful of the housing and unemployment problems that faced blacks in 1945. They were not
unaware of residual race prejudice towards blacks, perhaps
slightly reinvigorated by the many southern whites who were
also drawn to California during the war years. These optimistic
Californians thought that perhaps western prejudice had spent
itself on the Japanese, the Chinese, and the Mexicans. They also
saw that in the big cities of California the war years had produced (especially in 1945—the last year of the war) interracial
groups called Councils for Civic Unity. Readers with long memories may remember these councils in Los Angeles, San Francisco, Berkeley, and Oakland. They seemed to augur a healthy
interracial climate. The fact that the United Nations was organized in San Francisco seemed to cap this optimistic mood. In
November 1945 a special issue of the *Journal of Educational
Sociology* devoted to race relations on the Pacific Coast reflected
this optimistic mood, but it also emphasized obvious difficulties. It noted that already those blacks who were last hired had
been first fired. It pointed to the unrelieved housing shortage
and the rising practice of realtors and homeowner groups to
resist selling and renting homes to blacks, thus further "ghetto-
izing" already congested black communities. Into this environment a new generation of California blacks was born.

Perhaps the most ironic element of the journal's articles was the optimistic assessment of its most eminent contributor, Carey McWilliams, famous critic and writer. To him, the increased collaboration of white and black laborers, the potential alliance for the black and Mexican communities, the intensified activities on housing by the NAACP, and the white antiracist contingent in the Democratic Congress were hopes for optimism. (California congresswoman Helen Gahagan Douglas, a member of this wartime group, was the first *white* member of Congress to employ a black on a congressional staff in Washington.) Carey McWilliams wrote:

> It is my firm conviction that the Negro community in Los Angeles is destined to write a new chapter in the history of the Negro in urban communities in America. . . . [T]he pattern of race relations on the West Coast is in a state of flux. The situation is so fluid, in fact, that almost anything could happen.

McWilliams could hardly have predicted the shape and form in which events justified his comment that "almost anything could happen." While the basic ingredients of defeat and despair were being shaped for huge numbers of blacks in California in the postwar decade, the angry reaction and its crystallization into action would be triggered by developments outside the state.[1]

In 1954, nine years after the end of World War II, a signal for action came across the country from the national capital. The Supreme Court of the United States, as the result of a case initiated by the NAACP, handed down the now famous decision in *Brown* v. *Board of Education of Topeka,* which declared that separate was not equal. While this signal was directed to offending state and local governments in matters of education, it became in time a catalytic agent for the national protest movement that embraced the resentments of black people. This movement or, more accurately, these movements began in the East and Midwest and then quickly spread across the country as the civil rights movement. It had multiple origins, many of them in the South. Some authors trace its unique tactics of nonviolent civil disobedience to 1942 in Chicago. Inspired by the principles of nonviolence espoused by Mahatma Gandhi, a group of blacks and whites came together to form the Congress of Racial Equality, soon to be called simply CORE. During World War II it had successfully ended discriminatory practices in Chicago's restaurants in the downtown area. In the postwar period CORE had its ups and down in similar efforts in the South while gradually gaining a national reputation as a pacifist-type civil rights organization. The young activists of CORE received frequent legal aid from America's oldest civil rights organization, the National Association for the Advancement of Colored People.

In 1961, seven years after the *Brown* decision, CORE once again was in the forefront of the nonviolent civil rights struggle. In that year it initiated what became known as the "Freedom Ride," which sought to integrate terminals and waiting rooms everywhere in the South. The spectacle of black and white young men enduring the terror and beatings of racist whites all along their route captured the attention of the nation. When it was over, CORE was a household world. The suffering of these marchers revived moribund chapters of CORE and helped in the founding of new ones. By 1963 there were CORE chapters in the major cities of California and they were girding for action.

The civil rights revolution that began in Montgomery, Alabama, in 1955 under the leadership of the Reverend Martin Luther King, Jr., gradually spread north and west until it reached California in 1963 under the guidance of CORE. The young people of CORE were supported by other black and white organizations and especially by the NAACP, now compelled by the times to add street work to its court activities which in the past had been its most common arena for accomplishment. In 1963 CORE members went into the Los Angeles streets to protest housing discrimination and de facto segregation in the schools. Their tactics were nonviolent although they broke the peace.

CORE's struggle to end housing discrimination in southern California focused on Monterey Park, where a black physicist had been denied a home. After five weeks of agitation the venture ended successfully. CORE then joined with the NAACP in an attempt to break down housing barriers for middle-class blacks, but further conclusive victories eluded them. After the arrest of some demonstrators, a thousand people joined forces on a Saturday in the summer of 1963 and marched to a suburban subdivision of Los Angeles. In spite of this activity and support by the state attorney general, who enforced an injunction against one builder, the result was inconclusive. Some relief in the unbearable congestion in black communities was achieved, but de facto school segregation continued.

In San Francisco the work of CORE and its allies took on more dramatic forms. The movement was concerned about jobs, and in 1963 its members began picketing a restaurant chain called Mel's Drive-In to bring pressure for the hiring of blacks. This protest was followed the next year by an effort to get supermarkets to hire blacks. Shopping carts would be filled to overflowing with food, including frozen food items, taken to the front of the stores, and abandoned near the cash register. In that same year, 1964, the San Francisco chapter of CORE engaged in its most spectacular venture at gaining jobs for blacks. It took on the elegant Sheraton-Palace Hotel and the extensive auto row on Van Ness Avenue and borrowed the "sit-in" tactic successfully used in southern public facilities by the Student Non-Violent Coordinating Committee (SNCC) in the early 1960s. In both cases hundreds of young people sat down in these establishments until some commitment was made to hire blacks and, in some instances, they demanded that hiring go beyond just placing token blacks on the payroll. These protests made the front pages of major newspapers and often featured photos showing the police arresting and dragging out demonstrators.[2]

While these events publicized CORE's work, the movement also engaged the corporate structure when it went after the Bank of America in San Francisco and demanded that blacks be employed in the then lily-white world of banking. Today's young people who see minorities working as tellers in banks little realize that once it was not so. The immediate results of this dramatic movement by young blacks and their white allies was a ripple of tokenism in hiring minorities. But many occupational areas, including the crafts and building trades, had black employees for the first time.

The year 1963 was a national milestone in the civil rights movement. The highly visible March on Washington took place that year, an action that was a coalition of many organizations and drew to the nation's capital a quarter of a million blacks and whites. Here Martin Luther King made his now immortal speech, "I Have a Dream." The national attention was captured by these events. By this time the brutalities of southern life had become common knowledge to most Americans who watched on television the heavy hand of southern law enforcement officers towards civil rights workers. Many young people, especially students, black and white, were caught up in the enthusiasm of the movement. While these struggles of a lasting character took place, new dramatic scenarios of confrontation were being written with symbolic significance for black and white Californians. The conventional civil rights struggles were soon overshadowed by the black revolution, and some of the most dramatic scenes of this development occurred in California.

The brand of political nationalism represented by the Black Panthers was born in Oakland, California, in 1966. Its founders, Huey Newton and Bobby Seale, were young men who had spent their formative years in post–World War II Oakland where that city's black population was growing faster than the local institutions and economy could accommodate it. The city's police force found it especially difficult to adjust to the large influx of black migrants. Young blacks, in turn, felt particularly harassed by the Oakland police. In this setting the Black Panther party flourished. Radical in style and rhetoric, it called itself Marxist-Leninist. It published a weekly paper which carried local as well as national news, and in its first half-dozen years employed language and illustrations that left little doubt about the organization's deep hatred for the police. The drawings of the smoking end of a gun and a pig's head on a uniform were virtually the paper's trademark. The organization rapidly caught the imagination of inner-city young blacks and spread eastward to the Atlantic Coast.

Police confrontations quickly became the mark of Panther activity, and newspaper reportage obscured the fact that in most inner cities the police did not treat minority citizens with the deference with which they treated white citizens. The effect was a deep hatred of police by most blacks, and especially young blacks. The Panthers made popular the word "pig" as a substitute for the word "police" among blacks and white radicals. It was after bloody encounters with the police and the exposure in the 1970s of the FBI's attempts to destroy the Panther leadership that the Panthers moved into mainstream politics. The rhetoric softened, the guns became less visible, the *Black Panther* newspaper illustrations switched from smoking guns to pictures of black mothers, and in Oakland the Panther organization ran candidates for office and conducted free food centers. The organization's present direction is not clear, since its members are concerned with a variety of issues; and the remaining major leader is Huey Newton. Bobby Seale appears to be testing out new and traditional careers elsewhere in the United States.

Conventional black politics, though less colorful, consisted primarily of black Democrats pressing for additional black candidates in California elections. The most visible black in the state Assembly was Augustus Hawkins, who was first elected to that body in 1934; in 1948 he was joined by another black, William Byron Rumford, from the Berkeley-Oakland area. In 1962, two more blacks were elected from the Los Angeles area, F. Douglass Ferrell and Mervyn Dymally. In 1964, San Francisco elected Willie L. Brown, Jr., to the state Assembly. (It is worth noting that the two black assemblymen from the Bay area needed and received white votes to be elected.) In 1966, three more blacks were elected to the state Assembly from the Los Angeles area and one more from the Bay area: Yvonne Brathwaite Burke, Bill Green, and Leon Ralph from Los Angeles, and John Miller from Berkeley. This period of major entry into mainstream politics also saw Hawkins leave the Assembly after the 1962 elections to take a seat in the U.S. House of Representatives as the first black congressman from the West. All were Democrats and most of their elections reflected the great numerical increase of the postwar black population. The large black migrations of the 1940s and 1950s were now coming into their own politically and the actuality of black power in the conventional sense was gradually being realized. This development would continue and expand in the decades that followed.

In 1959, this power of blacks in California was recognized by Jesse Unruh, the Democratic Speaker of the Assembly, when he introduced a civil rights bill that was easily passed by the heavily Democratic state legislature and signed by Governor Edmund G. "Pat" Brown. This statute attempted to eliminate discrimination in housing and employment, but it left prosecution of violators to the expensive court process. For minority people of color, the cost of prosecution was a burden that they could not carry. William Byron Rumford then introduced a measure providing for the presentation of grievances to the State Fair Employment Practices Commission, a procedure much more within the reach of the poor. The Rumford bill became law in 1963, but the realtors of California immediately sought to overturn it by means of an initiative. Known as Proposition 14, the ballot measure became the hottest issue in the election campaign of 1964. Its proponents claimed that the main issue was the right of citizens to do what they wished with their property in the matter of selling or renting. Its opponents claimed that race prejudice and the rights of minorities to move where they pleased were the issues. In the fall elections, Proposition 14 won overwhelmingly and thus the Rumford Act was invalidated. Blacks and others read the returns as a naked manifestation of racism in California. However, a few years later Proposition 14 was overturned by the state supreme court (in *Reitman et al.* v. *Lincoln W. Mulkey*) and the Rumford Act was again in effect.

The consequences of this popular vote may never be completely known, though there were at least two significant events that might have been triggered by the statewide manifestation of racist attitudes. They were the organization of the Black Panther party in 1966, which has already been discussed, and the Watts riot. Hostility toward the police might alone have brought about a riot in Watts, but the passage of Proposition 14 could hardly have been oil on troubled waters.

The passage of Proposition 14 came at a crucial time when the value of integrating or allying with whites was being questioned by black activists. Racial friction within the civil rights movement became widespread during the Mississippi Freedom Summer project in 1964, and many black civil rights leaders felt betrayed when the 1964 Democratic National Convention refused to seat a black delegation from Mississippi. A year later, the civil rights movement would be overshadowed by the black revolution, which dramatically manifested itself in California.

For many blacks, whether in or out of the civil rights movement, life had changed during the period between the end of World War II and the beginning of the 1960s. Frustration and bitterness were becoming obvious to many. In California, the problems of decent housing, jobs (especially for youth), and police brutality were chronic. The continued migration of blacks to California increased the population density of already crowded black ghettos. Young blacks grew up separated from the larger white world, and their own world became one of de facto segregation with declining educational advantages.

In this decade of rising expectations, a long-muted sense of urgency came to the fore, especially among black youth who, in typical American fashion, demanded hurried satisfaction. A less typical ingredient, however, was their radical rhetoric. Even before the march on Washington, a black student movement emerged on southern campuses that allied itself for a time with Martin Luther King's Southern Christian Leadership Conference. It was called the Student Non-Violent Coordinating Committee (SNCC). Early in the 1960s, SNCC moved in a radical direction, rapidly shedding its pacifist image and gradually developing an antiwhite posture. In 1966 SNCC's best-known spokesman, Stokely Carmichael, uttered for the first time the slogan "Black Power," which had an electrifying effect on the masses of black youth around the country, especially in the urban centers. SNCC's radicalism was shared by CORE, which began manifesting the same militancy and rhetoric. An illustration of the new mood was the contemptuous rejection of the word "Negro" and the demand that only "black" be used to refer to Afro-Americans.[3] Those young blacks who wished to denigrate "Negro" did not know that during the years of American slavery many slaveowners referred to their slaves as "my blacks."

The new mood introduced another new phrase, "black nationalism." What is now clear in retrospect is that black power and black nationalism meant different things to different blacks. This is well illustrated by what happened in California beginning in the 1950s.

The Black Muslims, who were not in the mainstream of black nationalism, were a thoroughly separatist and nationalist religious group which had adopted the religion of the Arab world. They achieved a reputation for puritanical living and gained converts, to the astonishment of many, among black prison inmates. Their success was partly due to the charismatic figure of Malcolm X, who had himself once been a convict, and partly to the customs and symbols of Islam. Malcolm X's influence may explain Eldridge Cleaver's temporary conversion, which occurred while Cleaver was in jail. The Muslims, who had midwestern origins, grew rapidly in Los Angeles and San Francisco after World War II. They believed in economic self-sufficiency and ignored politics. Under their leadership many Muslim-owned businesses were founded and thrived in urban centers in California.

The main strength of the Muslims lay in the young black migrants of the post–World War II period who were facing the new frustrations of northern and western life. While older California blacks remained attached to their Christian black churches and generally ignored the Muslims, in the postwar years young blacks in and out of the Muslim movement were attracted to Malcolm X. The vividness of his antiwhite oratory and call for blacks to separate from whites in their struggles for black security and dignity profoundly influenced the membership of both CORE and SNCC. In the California chapters of these two organizations, as in the chapters elsewhere in the nation, the pressures led to memberships that were exclusively black. In deep disappointment and in some cases anger, radical and liberal whites left SNCC and CORE. Older black organizations also lamented this development with its antiwhite rhetoric only to earn the caustic criticism of the younger groups. The resulting split in black leadership had a profound effect upon the fortunes of the movement.

In August 1965 during one of the warmest summers in Los Angeles, the black community of Watts exploded into California's most devastasting racial incident. It was a six-day disaster during which nearly ten thousand blacks took to the streets, looted stores, burned cars, beat whites, and killed (or caused to be killed) thirty-four persons. The businesses that were destroyed were mostly white-owned; the people who died were mostly black. Ironically, a year before this event the Urban League had judged Los Angeles the most desirable city for blacks. The subsequent McCone Commission Report on this riot as well as on other outbreaks made it clear that housing, unemployment, and police brutality were major causes of unrest. Of equal interest are the claims that this explosion was a release from boredom and the expression of an end, if temporarily, of powerlessness.[4] The McCone Commission made the pioneering suggestion that compensatory programs for blacks be substituted for the slow-moving "equality of opportunity"–type job programs. Beyond that, the Commission had few other suggestions and, according to Bayard Rustin, a long-time national black leader, was even superficial in its analysis of the roots of the riot. Yet Los Angeles Mayor Samuel Yorty and Governors Edmund (Pat) Brown and, later, Ronald Reagan, as well as the city council, legislature, and a mix of Democrats and Republicans, did practically nothing in trying to change conditions in Watts. Only the federal government initiated programs in Watts that affected a small percentage of the community's population.[5] Officials generally seemed unable to cope with the problems raised by this disaster.

On the campuses of California's many colleges and high schools in the 1960s a phase of this nationalist movement appeared among the then increasing number of blacks attending school. This aspect of nationalism took the form of Black Student Unions (BSUs). Throughout California, and especially on campuses in or near large black communities, BSU chapters became springboards for a variety of campaigns. The most common scholastic demand was for a Black Studies program in a Black Studies Department controlled by blacks and taught by blacks. The rationale for such a program, which had genuine merit but was seriously questioned by administrations and faculty, was the incontrovertible fact that the Afro-American and his part in American history had often been weakly presented by American educators. Questions quickly arose, however, over who would teach these courses and who would hire the teachers, and would teachers have to be black. What complicated the problem from campus to campus in California, as well as elsewhere in the nation, was the fact that few academics had specific preparation to teach such courses. While southern black colleges had been offering Afro-American courses for decades and had talent enough for their own purposes, they were unable suddenly to provide teachers for other institutions.

The campaign for black studies moved across nearly every college campus in the state and brought the establishment of a wide variety of programs in quality and style. Much struggle and grief arose over the issue of course content and staffing, powers that administrations were reluctant to surrender. This authority, however, was demanded by the most militant and nationalist blacks, who believed it was essential to their struggle for "the control of their destinies."

The older generation of black leaders from the NAACP and Urban League, as well as the established black scholars in black and white universities, were uneasy over these developments. They warned against black studies programs that were designed as "party lines" for individual sects of black radicals that were activist-oriented rather than scholarship-oriented. In addition, they were alarmed at the possibility that the rush to staff these programs would result in poorly prepared teachers, who, in their wish to be fashionable, would not recognize the difference between balanced information and impassioned harangue. This older generation was also concerned that the programs would be so totally antiwhite as to become, in fact, a reverse racism.

The results of this struggle are still obscured by controversy and contradictory opinion. So many of the leading figures, black and white, have left the stage of this drama (according to Robert Brustein of Yale University, the movement had the quality of theatre)[6] that factual assessments are now hard to find. Tentative observations suggest that at the best-known institutions the tone for the black studies programs was set by the most militant blacks who were often inexperienced with or ignorant of scholarly standards. On some campuses white and black scholars had already been teaching black history courses before the demand came from the BSUs, but white instructors were rarely encouraged to teach in the programs.

A classic case of confrontation occurred at San Francisco State University (then College) in 1968. The Black Student Union presented the administration with ten nonnegotiable demands which put blacks in essential control of every aspect of the black studies program. For any college administration this demand was an unprecedented example of arrogance, but when the smoke cleared, the BSU seemed to have what it wanted. The San Francisco administration retained, however, the power of granting tenure to faculty in the black studies division. This power was apparently retained by most other school administrations in California. With the passage of time it appears that this withholding of tenure contributed to the instability of the black studies faculty. During the early and hurried years of these programs some of the teachers were persons of minimal qualifications who obtained positions because they were highly visible in the rhetorical aspects of the struggle. Many of them eventually were denied tenure.

Another California college campus in the 1960s was the setting for an important aspect of the black movement — the "revolt" of the black athletes. The catalyst for this movement was Harry Edwards, a sociology professor at San Jose State University. In 1967 he and a number of world-class athletes talked about boycotting the 1968 Olympics. The idea had been suggested by black comedian Dick Gregory a few years earlier as a means of protesting the racist treatment of black athletes at collegiate levels as well as at the Olympics. A dramatic meeting on the San Jose campus developed into a broader one in Los Angeles. Athletes such as Tommie Smith and Lou Alcindor (Kareem Abdul-Jabbar) were present to support a boycott. The idea, after much debate, was discarded, and the militant black athletes who competed in Mexico City in 1968 manifested their protest against racism in various ways, including the raising of the black-gloved clenched fist, photos of which appeared on the front pages of the world's press. The nation was both shocked and sobered by the unpatriotic actions, but the white majority was angry. In the years that followed, racism in American athletics showed evidence of decline without disappearing.[7]

By the end of the 1960s, there were offerings of black studies in most institutions of higher learning and in many high schools. On this issue the Black Student Unions attained a degree of success in their confrontation with white-controlled administrations. Some of these administrators were ready to see the logic of black studies while others were frightened into granting the demands. Many black and some white teachers of American history became instructors in black history courses. The demand at all levels for black studies programs came with such speed and force, as far as school administrations were concerned, that the graduate schools were caught unprepared.

In southern California the control of the black studies program became a power struggle at UCLA between noncampus groups of black nationalists, the "US" led by Ron Karenga, then a cultural black nationalist, and the Black Panthers, who were political nationalists. The cultural black nationalists believed that the strength-giving ingredient for Afro-Americans was a strong identification with African culture. Therefore, they felt American history and politics to be a waste of time. The political nationalists believed in gaining control of all aspects of black life, including political, educational, and economic institutions, especially those controlled by whites in the black communities. In 1969, these two views and their respective organizations clashed on the UCLA campus. Two deaths took place on the campus and four more off campus. Many serious charges have been made; not least is the one that the FBI was aware of these hates and manipulated them to provoke the murders. The U.S. Senate Select Committee on Intelligence revealed information from FBI files which showed that the FBI encouraged the battle between US and the Panthers by fabricating insulting cartoons of the Panthers, presumably done by US, and by sending provocative anonymous letters to leaders of both groups designed to stimulate trouble between them. [8]

Other developments involving California blacks (as well as whites) were associated with the militants and left-wing groups. Some of these events were then high drama, but now are difficult to measure in terms of popular support by blacks in the state. They involved the activities of concerned blacks and whites who joined in a movement to publicize the lives of blacks in prisons. A few of these blacks quickly became the center of much attention, none more so than George Jackson, whose prison writings were widely read. His trials and experiences also received special attention from Angela Davis, a young black philosopher and lecturer who was well known at this time as an avowed Marxist. Her presence on the UCLA faculty caused an uproar in the press, leading to her eventual dismissal as an instructor.

In 1970 in a courthouse in San Rafael, Marin County, George Jackson's younger brother, Jonathan, and several blacks attempted to rescue some black prisoners in the courtroom. The event had many aspects of a wild west scenario. They took white hostages with them in order to bargain for the freedom of George Jackson. The effort ended in disaster, with several whites and blacks dead, including young Jackson. It was alleged that Angela Davis had supplied Jackson with guns, knowing they would be used in the Marin courthouse. She suddenly disappeared but was captured in the East months later. There ensued a tremendous campaign in California and throughout the country to free her, in which the small Communist party and the Black Panthers participated. She was a member of both organizations. After a trial in San Jose, she was acquitted. George Jackson, in a cloudy series of events, was later killed in a shootout in jail in what some charged was a planned assassination.

The final high-drama event of black-white radicalism was the bizarre story of the Symbionese Liberation Army (SLA). In late 1973 this small group of fanatics, led by a black named Cinque (although most SLA members were radical whites), murdered the very popular black Oakland superintendent of schools, Marcus Foster. They charged Foster with "selling out" blacks. Testimony to the degree to which the SLA was out of touch with reality was the fact that the whole spectrum of black opinion in California, not to mention white, was outraged by the murder. In February 1974 the SLA made international news headlines by kidnapping Patricia Hearst, a member of the famous Hearst newspaper family. The SLA used her to compel the Hearst family to give away millions of dollars worth of food to the black poor in the Bay area. The SLA's requirements for distribution required such speed that careful organization was not possible. The result was a degrading spectacle of hundreds of blacks who wildly grabbed for the food, which was at times thrown to them by young blacks who had broken from the crowd, jumped onto the food trucks, and hurled it to the people below.

While these dramatic scenarios of confrontation were being played out with their symbolic significance for white and black Californians, less volatile developments were taking place that would have consequences of more lasting character. Between 1960 and 1970 the state's black population grew from nearly 900,000 to 1,400,000. A charismatic black, the tall and slim Ronald Dellums, who had served on the Berkeley city council, ran for Congress in 1970 as a Democrat and, with the voting power given him by the coalitions of blacks and whites created during the Free Speech Movement in Berkeley, won a seat as the second California black in the House of Representatives. Dellums came by his leadership abilities naturally. His father and uncle were active members of the pioneering black union, the Brotherhood of Sleeping Car Porters. Two years later, Yvonne Burke left her seat in the California Assembly to run successfully for a congressional seat in Washington, where she joined the two other California members of the black contingent there. That same year, 1972, Julian Dixon took Burke's place in the Assembly, and still another new black appeared in the Assembly from the Los Angeles area, Frank Holloman. In 1974, Mervyn Dymally left the Assembly to become lieutenant governor under Edmund G. (Jerry) Brown, Jr.

However, Dymally was not the first black to win statewide office in California. In 1971 Wilson Riles ran an exciting race against Max Rafferty, a very conservative incumbent, and won the influential office of state superintendent of public instruction in California. While it was a hard-fought contest, Riles preferred to consider his post nonpartisan and himself an educator. His record of achievement over many years of service confirmed the voters' choice.

Such efforts at black power also achieved results in city elections. Cities such as Richmond, San Bernardino, Oakland, Berkeley, Seaside, and Stockton were electing black city councilmen, and in Berkeley black Warren Widener was elected mayor in 1971. In Los Angeles, where blacks cast seventeen percent of the votes, former police officer and city councilman Thomas (Tom) Bradley became mayor in 1973. Born on a cotton farm in Texas, Bradley and his parents had moved to Los Angeles when he was a child. Upon graduation from high school, he entered UCLA on an athletic scholarship and later, while working in the police department, earned a law degree. His election victory over the incumbent mayor Samuel Yorty was marked by the largest white vote for a black candidate in any American city. His great popularity as mayor brought repeated reelection but not higher political offices, although he was favorably regarded as a vice presidential candidate in 1984. In 1973 the largely black city of Compton saw Doris A. Davis elected mayor. In the Bay area a second black mayor was elected in 1977 when Lionel Wilson gained that office in Oakland through a coalition of conservative and radical blacks, most particularly the Panthers. The list of blacks holding elective public office as judges and members of boards of education as well as lawmakers is extensive and can best be appreciated by a glance at the latest edition of the *National Roster of Black Elected Officials.*

In spite of the surge of black elected officials in the 1960s and 1970s, one should remember that none of these twentieth-century personalities was the first black elected to office in California. Nearly a hundred years earlier, in 1888, Edward Duplex, a New Haven, Connecticut, gold-rush-era migrant, was elected the mayor of the little town of Wheatland in Yuba County. He was the town barber and a statewide leader of the Colored Convention Movement from the 1850s to the 1870s.[9] However, the election of Duplex in Wheatland reflected the comfortable and trusting intimacy of a small town in nineteenth-century America where people knew their neighbors and where the stakes of power were minimal. The highly visible presence of powerful black political personalities in California nearly a hundred years after Duplex represents an entirely different set of circumstances. In most cases, the elected black politicians reflect a conscious and organized expression of democratic representation. Several of these black politicians were part of remarkable white-black-brown interracial coalitions, notably headed by Tom Bradley of Los Angeles, who in 1984 was reelected to an unprecedented fourth term.

Paradoxically, these political victories gradually brought the public mind to the realization that an electoral victory leaves many painful problems unsolved. While a black middle and upper class is clearly emerging in the post–World War II United States, a very large number of Afro-Americans remain in poverty. The chasm between the upwardly mobile blacks and their immobile brothers and sisters widens, and the poverty of the underclass is not only the problem of California but also of the rest of the nation.

CHAPTER SIX

The Uncertain Seventies and Eighties

THE YEARS BETWEEN the gold rush of 1849 and the 1980s had wrought great changes in the Afro-American communities of California. For decades the number of blacks hovered at about one percent of the state's population. In the twentieth century it rose slowly until by 1980, following accelerated growth, it was close to eight percent. In the nineteenth century black males had persistently outnumbered black females, but in the 1980s balance has occurred. In fact, black women slightly outnumber men in the 1980 census. What has persisted is the tendency for blacks to avoid agricultural labor. They became a city people even in counties where the cities were small. Although there always were some black farm owners, they have remained few; in 1970 California blacks of all ages and both sexes classified as rural totaled slightly more than 35,000 out of a total black population of 1,400,000. In 1980, when the black population was closer to 2,000,000, the census recorded only 14,000 employed in agriculture, forestry, or fishing.[1]

For decades, even when blacks were relatively numerous, they were the "invisible people," but that too has changed in California as elsewhere. White racism has weakened, but it continues in subtle and unconscious ways. As a result, the 1970s constituted a decade of both progress and poverty for California blacks. Some of the most conspicuous events of the

1960s — ghetto riots, black nationalist movements, civil rights demonstrations — had ended by 1970 or would fade from the California and national scenes early in the decade. But the basic condition of a black population largely confined to a few communities persisted, and out of this situation arose several problems whose solutions would either be more baffling or controversial than were those of equal opportunity in employment and housing and better police relations. Solutions were complicated by honest as well as dishonest differences among people of all colors.

Poverty as a fundamental problem was hardly new to black communities. But it assumed new characteristics as the black population nationally and in California specifically divided into divergent lower, middle, and upper classes. In the 1970s, an unprecedented number of blacks advanced in educational, economic, and occupational status into the middle class and often into the mainstream of American society. Their successes will be noted later in this chapter. But nearly half the blacks nationwide (and probably a similar percentage in California) remained in a condition of poverty or near-poverty and collectively came to be referred to as the underclass.

The presence of this large underclass at a time when an apparently permanent middle- and upper-class black segment is becoming more visible has produced some new thinking about class and race. The black scholar William J. Wilson, in his *The Declining Significance of Race* (2nd ed., University of Chicago Press, 1980), contended that public policy should shift from treating black poverty as a racial issue to seeing it as a class issue. His position has not gone unchallenged, and there are those who fear that his views may be manipulated by those who pretend that racism has ceased to exist. Wilson does not claim that racism is dead, but feels that in turn its overemphasis can result in neglect of those suffering from poverty.

Perhaps the most serious aspect of poverty had exploded on the national scene in 1965 when a report on the black family was made to the President by Daniel Patrick Moynihan, later to be U.S. senator from New York. The burden of this report was that the black family in the northern urban slums had been deeply affected by disintegrating factors, economic and social, which deserved as much federal concern as civil rights. Worry about black families in the urban slums was hardly a new subject, but an unexpectedly sharp negative reaction to Moynihan's report was registered by many black leaders. In retrospect, it appears that the negative reaction was not about the details of the report but rather the purposes to which such a report might lend itself in hostile hands. The year 1965 was a sensitive time when "Black Is Beautiful" was a reigning slogan with black activists. Young black males were strident in their language of black pride and black power. Moynihan's report, with its realistic message of matriarchal families and black male neglect of these families, collided sharply with the prouder messages of black militancy.[2]

Little mention of the family as a problem had been made by California blacks during the nineteenth century. Family life was then discernible, as nearly four hundred black school-age children attended segregated schools. The details of this black family life become blurred before the twentieth century, but the census reports suggest that the children came mostly from families that had both a father and a mother present. The two post–Civil War Negro newspapers of San Francisco lavishly reported the social life of the black community, but family life itself was not a feature of black or white journalism. Again the census reports that before the twentieth century these families lived in relatively integrated neighborhoods where most of the lower-class people lived. The social life of the unmarried black males, who were still a considerable majority in the nineteenth century, is well described in Douglass H. Daniel's *Pioneer Urbanites,* which relates the saloon and social-club life of black San Francisco.

During the Progressive Era, there were occasional indications of social problems related to family within California black communities. Several black women's organizations founded in the early 1900s, such as the Sojourner Truth Industrial Club of Los Angeles, were expressly oriented toward wayward children, usually girls. Prostitution received considerable editorial attention from the black press. Charlotta Bass of the *California Eagle* particularly attacked the practice of locating red-light districts in Negro residential areas.[3] The Los Angeles Forum and much of the black press frequently spoke of the need to suppress the "vicious element" and "keep newcomers to our city in the proper channels for its moral uplift." But there was little mention of basic instability within large numbers of black families, nor would there be until well after World War II.

When Moynihan's report was released, it caused considerable debate over the origins and causes of black family instability. For several years, historic forces, particularly slavery, were emphasized and criticized. By the middle of the 1970s, however, the dominant factor was thought to be the dual environment of ghetto and poverty, and some particular features of the black population. California blacks on the whole tended to be slightly younger than the general population. Their families were larger than white families, and Negro mothers usually had their children earlier in life. These children attended schools that were older, larger, and more crowded. In addition, they lived in crowded housing conditions that were less adequate than white housing conditions even where blacks lived in largely single-family dwellings.[4] Little realized by whites as well as by black Californians is the extent to which single- and two-family dwellings in poor areas are a uniquely California phenomenon. California-born black students who have visited New York and Chicago have experienced culture shock at seeing the huge multidwelling apartment houses, many stories high, in which densely packed black families live. As early as the years just before World War I many blacks in California had become accustomed to dwellings like those in the Oakland picture on page 31. But by the 1960s this picture was deceptively idyllic. Most of the single-family dwellings were inhabited by more than one family. Not only were these houses overcrowded, but the communities also suffered from a lack of public facilities.

The crisis of the black family had become so acute by 1984 that a Summit Conference of Black Organizations on the Black Family was convened at Fisk University in Nashville, Tennessee. The organizers of the conference were spurred by the fact that in 1970 thirty-one percent of black families in the United States had been headed by women and that ten years later this figure had risen to forty-two percent. While specific percentages for California are not easily available, one can assume that the national figures apply to the state. It is known that in 1960 over twenty percent of black families in the West were headed by women. The data of the Summit Conference suggest that female-headed black families in the Bay area and in Los Angeles in 1980 must also be close to forty percent. Of equal concern to the conference sponsors was the continuing growth in the number of young unwed mothers. In 1979 the majority of black infants were the children of single women.[5]

As indicated earlier, the children of these families, whether from single or two-parent families, attend older and more crowded schools. The locations of these schools were — and remain — overwhelmingly in economically depressed areas that have become all-black communities. Whether intentional or not, school segregation followed from the housing pattern. This separateness produced inequality and out of it came the desegregation movements in California.

Efforts at desegregating Los Angeles schools in 1968 gained national attention. They came about because the American Civil Liberties Union (ACLU) entered the desegregation struggle and filed a suit in the name of a Mary Crawford. This produced in 1970 the widely publicized decision of Judge Alfred Gitelson and led to the busing of students. Negative reactions came swiftly from Mayor Samuel Yorty, Governor Ronald Reagan, and even President Richard M. Nixon. Los Angeles school officials claimed that busing 240,000 children would cost annually forty million dollars. While the ACLU disputed this figure, the decision was challenged in higher courts. In the meantime, the mounting hostility toward Judge Gitelson brought his defeat for reelection.[6]

The antibusing momentum in Los Angeles continued through the rest of the decade, and in 1979 a recall movement ousted the Los Angeles school board president who favored a general busing program. That same year an antibusing leader replaced him in a special election. Also in 1979, California voted two to one for a state constitutional amendment that forbade any busing that was done to end de facto discrimination. This meant that busing could only occur where it could be proven that school segregation had been deliberately sought rather than a result of "accidental" circumstances. As a result, the amount of busing fell to an ineffective minimum.

However, it is likely that a thoroughgoing busing program might have failed because of other developments. The city of Los Angeles covers a large area, and travel within its boundaries is difficult. The vast growth of suburbs in southern California was as much a white flight from the inner city as it was population growth. While well-to-do blacks were also moving to the suburbs, their numbers were not large enough to produce a significant by-product in integrated education. As a result, in the Los Angeles school district, the number of white students had dropped to a fourth of the entire student body by 1980. Without enough white students to put into the mix, integration through busing appeared to be less and less reasonable.

One can be certain, however, that as long as blacks feel that separateness represents inequality, and the evidence still supports that view, sympathy for the desegregation struggle will continue. It will end when blacks feel, as white minorities felt in many eastern big cities in the past, that the preponderance of their particular ethnic group in any school is simply a sign of residence and not discrimination.

The tide of rising expectations among blacks in the 1960s swept through all phases of American life, eventually reaching the exclusive world of the medical schools. In 1969 this movement brought about an affirmative action program in student admissions at the medical school on the Davis campus of the University of California. Under this program sixteen admissions were reserved for minority students out of a hundred openings each year. Allan Bakke, a white civil engineer in his thirties, applied for admission to the medical school in 1973 and again in 1974 and was rejected both times. He concluded that he had been discriminated against because he was white and that he would have been admitted but for the medical school's affirmative action program.

Bakke took his case to the courts, where his position was upheld by the California supreme court. At issue was the constitutionality of the Davis affirmative action program. Among blacks there was divided counsel on whether the university should defend its affirmative action program before the Supreme Court of the United States. They rightly feared that a negative decision by the court, which was widely regarded as a conservative court, would have harmful effects on affirmative action programs throughout the nation. In the end the university appealed to the highest court in the land. After a period of intense uneasiness marked by many demonstrations against

Bakke in California as well as across the nation, the U.S. Supreme Court in June 1978 handed down a five-to-four decision in favor of Allan Bakke. At the same time, however, the court softened its decision with kind words for affirmative action programs. Such programs would remain legal so long as race was not the sole criterion in granting admission. The court decision put Bakke into medical school and raised the issue of fairness in the admissions process. Whether it has kept blacks out of medical schools and comparable professional institutions remains to be seen. The admissions policies of the major professional centers of learning will reveal the true meaning of the Bakke decision.

Black scholar William Julius Wilson was critical of the energy spent on the Bakke case. That energy, he contended, would have been better spent winning approval of the Humphrey-Hawkins Bill, which was being debated in Congress at the time. That bill, if enacted, would have provided a long-range federal program to combat unemployment and underemployment. Such a program would have dealt with the black underclass with which Wilson remains primarily concerned.

While controversies continue, black cultural visibility rises. Afro-American communities in the state support more than two dozen locally published newspapers. Under various names, Afro-American historical societies have been organized, largely with middle-class black support. In Oakland, a well-publicized annual event called Black Film Makers Hall of Fame was organized in the 1970s to bring together national black film talent and honor distinguished performers in much the same manner as Hollywood honors its own in the "Oscar" and "Emmy" award ceremonies.

Only slightly less visible than these glamor events was the almost three hundred percent increase in the number of black school teachers, administrators, and other professionals between 1960 and 1970. The black college student population registered a sharp rise in the same decade. Californians were probably most aware of the black presence through blacks' entry into every home by way of television commercials and the daily presence of many highly visible newscasters. Currently, however, there is mounting criticism by such organizations as the NAACP of the roles that blacks get in television.

Among the stars who enjoy the glitter of the theater, sports, and politics are a considerable number of black Californians. Their performances give pride to the Afro-Americans in the state and evoke admiration from the white community. This is dramatically noticeable in the field of sports. As early as World War I a black, Walter Gordon, became a great football star at the University of California. In the World War II era Jackie Robinson, formerly an athlete at UCLA, made baseball history when he became the first black player in the major leagues. In the last few decades, the number of black California sports stars has become almost too large to count.

Black success in athletic endeavors has become a tremendous goal for black youth. Every school field, every recreation center is filled with black youths practicing their sport. They try to emulate their idols' rise to positions of eminence in professional sports with its too often elusive fame and financial success. Many wise heads have warned these black youth to look elsewhere for their long-range goals since the percentage of those who "make it" in professional sports is minuscule. Too many young college men, for example, have a brief period of glory and then wind up academically unprepared for rewarding lifetime pursuits; even worse, many athletes do not graduate from college.

The overemphasis on sports obscures the need for trained black professionals in medicine and education. The world of engineering and architecture is also too white. But the greatest need is for many more blacks in the most active and stable parts of the American economy. Here, California blacks, with few exceptions, are generally behind, as they are in the rest of the economy. Black businesses have achieved an uncertain foothold in spite of some notable successes in the insurance and undertaking sectors. They are still struggling for survival in the construction industry in spite of some assistance from the federally funded Small Business Administration (SBA). Looming in the background are the great numbers of teenage and young blacks without skills or satisfying employment. The aftermath of the Watts riot produced many programs that did some good, but when viewed in perspective, they did not draw enough blacks in trade and technical schools, much less professional schools.

The long-range value of the SBA to black business still remains to be assessed. Information is fragmentary and breakdowns of California data are inconclusive. In an April 1, 1978, *New Republic* article on the SBA, the writer thought the benefits to blacks were clouded by reports that some black businesses received loans they did not need, while other black businesses needed loans and did not obtain them. Furthermore, there is troubling evidence that black firms are often fronts for white businesses which use this device to get federal aid. Such criticism may be of minor importance since these firms do employ blacks.

Of greater importance to black businesses is the impact of national policies in many forms. Many black businesses depend upon their customers using food stamps, but during the 1980s the food-stamp program dropped several million persons from eligibility. Since people must eat, sales continue but are reduced. The variety of foods and the amounts reflect diminished purchasing power. The recession of 1981–1982 also imperiled black small businesses, and their ability to get loans from banks was nearly destroyed. Furthermore, the high interest rates for small businessmen with a narrow margin of profit makes borrowing, even if obtainable, pointless. An equally heavy recent blow to black small business was the cut in 1981 of about a billion dollars from the budget of the Small Business Administration. Parren Mitchell, chairman of the House Small Business Committee, predicted that one out of five minority businesses would fail without special help. A fourth of these businesses are in California. One expert in the Bay area predicted in 1982 that some 75 to 100 black-owned businesses would fail and 800 to 1,200 employees would lose their jobs. His prediction seems to be verified by unemployment statistics.[7]

By comparison with white-controlled business in California, the black presence is minuscule. But compared with Afro-American business in the rest of the nation, California blacks have an impressive record. The earliest major business venture to gain prominence in the black world is the Los Angeles–based Golden State Mutual Insurance Company, founded in 1925. It weathered the depression of the thirties and stands today as an enduring object of pride in black free enterprise. In the 1960s and 1970s other even more successful black businesses emerged

in California and were located in the centers of black population. Most of these were in automotive sales and services. In the
1970s Motown Industries moved from Detroit to Los Angeles
and enjoyed an enormous growth as an arm of the entertain-
ment industry. In 1982 Motown emerged as the second largest
black-owned business in the United States. It continued to hold
this position in 1984 with a sales record of $137 million.

However, as dramatic as the picture is for Motown's income,
there exists a paradox for black employment in California.
Golden State Mutual Insurance with an impressive income, but
not enough to qualify it for including in the 1985 roster of "Top
100 Black Businesses" in the national periodical *Black Enterprise,* employs almost the same number of blacks in California as
Motown Industries (about 200). Furthermore, while the 1982
census reports California as leading the nation in black businesses, 91 percent of these (44,000) are overwhelmingly "mom
and pop" businesses. Only 9 percent have salaried employees,
some of whom are not black.

While black business is most numerous and visible in southern California, northern California has its proportion, and some
of these businesses have qualified for the "top 100." One highly
visible achievement of black free enterprise, although not in the
"top 100," is the attractive Vanguard office building on Van Ness
Avenue near the Opera Plaza complex in San Francisco.[8]

In California one sees the gradual move of black business
away from insurance companies and undertaking establishments
to new fields of endeavor in the automotive world and the
building and construction industry. But these efforts are still
struggling for stability, and the total of these activities only
involves a fraction of the black labor force.

California blacks face another awkward job problem that
seems to be most aggravating in southern California. This problem has its roots in the legal and illegal migration of peoples
from Asia, Mexico, and Central America. The 1960s and 1970s
arrivals were very frequently middle-class persons who had fled
radical changes in their homelands and brought with them
business skills and money to invest. When locating in black
neighborhoods, they often employed their own nationals or
illegal aliens.

A striking case of conflict between local black job seekers and a nonwhite-owned firm occurred in Compton, an eighty percent black municipality in Los Angeles County. There the Hitachi Consumer Products Company, a Japanese-owned firm, opened a plant that hired primarily Asians and illegal aliens and thus gave no relief to black unemployment in Compton. The Hitachi Company was taken to the state Fair Employment and Housing Department where a settlement was reached. Black applicants who applied to Hitachi for jobs between January and October 1981 received damages in cash. The total amount was $250,000. Hitachi was also to initiate an affirmative action hiring program. For romantics who believed that brotherhood comes naturally to all nonwhite peoples, such events are hard to accept. But, in the words of the president of the Urban League of Los Angeles, "At a time when unemployment is at a record high and with black opportunities being eroded on all fronts, it is difficult to stand up and cheer these new citizens." He went on to say, "At times it appears that our government leaders give a higher priority to welcoming new immigrants than to helping those folks who are already here." His worry about unfair competition was also expressed by Wendell Green, the vice chairman of a black organization called the Committee for Representative Government, who addressed a hearing of the House Select Committee on Immigration and Refugee Policy that was held in Los Angeles in 1980. Blacks in the construction and garment industries, he said, were losing their jobs to Mexicans, and he was apprehensive about creating tensions between the blacks and Hispanics. "We have not spoken out before because we are extremely hesitant to become allies with bigots and racists." But speak out he did.[9]

Black-Asian relations had several other complications. These were highlighted in a front-page series in the *Los Angeles Sentinel,* a black weekly newspaper, during August-September 1983. The series revealed that Koreans were replacing black and white small businesses when the proprietors retired or sold out. The writer blamed the financial system for the situation because Koreans apparently had easier ways of securing credit. In providing loans, it was alleged, the local Korean-owned bank charged Koreans a lower rate of interest than was available to blacks who might have been interested in buying the businesses. The writer of the series also complained about the cour-

tesy of the shopkeepers. Black customers at these Korean-
owned retail shops, service stations, and liquor stores, he stated,
received rude treatment that smacked of antiblack racism. The
writer reported the development of black community organizations aimed at resisting these practices. A hopeful sign was the
request by a local Korean editor to reprint the series in his
newspaper. [10]

Tensions such as these have marked Afro-American and Asian
relations in the past. As far back as the mid-1860s, when the
railroads chose to employ Chinese laborers, blacks were unhappy
that freed slaves were not given these jobs. In those years blacks
also shied away from including the Chinese in their concerns
about discrimination in education. An experience with some
Japanese just before World War II highlighted the ways in
which the solution of one problem can become the setting for
the surfacing of another. Roi Ottley, a black journalist, tells the
ironic story of a group of Japanese developers who had obtained
a tract of land in Los Angeles for home development only to find
their efforts blocked on racial grounds by nearby whites. The
Japanese rallied black support in a struggle against these whites.
The Japanese developers won and were allowed to proceed, but
the new housing area was subsequently restricted against black
occupancy. In another context, Afro- and Japanese-American
relations were much closer. When the Japanese were evacuated
from Los Angeles (their community was called "Little Tokyo"),
the evacuation center was the setting for black husbands visiting their Japanese wives. Incidentally, after the forced departure of Japanese from "Little Tokyo," this area became a black
neighborhood. [11]

The complaint that nonblack small businessmen treat blacks
unfeelingly and with racist overtones has been heard for decades
from inhabitants of densely populated black urban areas. As a
result a campaign for blacks to own businesses in their own
communities began in recent years with much pressure applied
to the franchise food industry. Organizations such as People
United to Save Humanity (PUSH) and the NAACP are in the
forefront of this movement. As a consequence some gains have
been made, but most recently the franchise story has taken a
surprising twist. Black entrepreneurs have emerged who are not
happy with being limited to franchises in black neighborhoods.

They claim that vandalism and persistent robbery cause their security costs to soar. Consequently they are asking for franchises in white neighborhoods. For example, Charles Griffis, who came to California from Michigan in 1977, owned four McDonald's franchises in Los Angeles by 1984. All were in black or mixed neighborhoods, and he demanded franchises in white districts. Company policy, however, opposed his wishes. In the words of the *New York Times* (March 12, 1984): "McDonald's says it is being sensitive to black leaders' requests when it sends black business people into inner city neighborhoods, but Mr. Griffis says that sensitivity confines him and other black business people to the ghetto." The manner in which this paradoxical question will be resolved remains to be seen.

To encourage blacks to stand upon their own feet, to avoid the temptation of shortcuts to wealth, and to safeguard their integrity, the Reverend Jesse Jackson, the charismatic black leader of PUSH, conducted in the 1970s an inspirational program throughout the nation to persuade young blacks to develop basic skills, regardless of real or fancied obstacles. His slogan was "Black Is Dutiful." However, if the controlling forces of white and black society do not provide the material and psychological underpinnings to his efforts, his work will produce meager results. *Newsweek* reported in August 1975 that, by conservative estimate ten years after the Watts riot, forty percent of young blacks in the area were unemployed. They were without work in spite of an expenditure of four hundred million dollars in Watts which produced a long-needed medical center, an industrial park (the largest plant there employs 250 workers), some government buildings, and a few supermarkets.

The dramatic mix of achievements and failures brings to mind a metaphor from the writing of Negro author Saunders Redding. ("Negro" is what he calls himself with pride.) He compares blacks in the United States to a people traveling down a road covered with an oil slick on which traction is hard to achieve. In retrospect, we can see that the struggle of the sixties removed much of that slick, but for blacks to achieve a parity of opportunity with whites calls for more of the "slick" to be removed.

CHAPTER SEVEN

Some Areas
of Progress

T HE VICTORY OF the property tax initiative, Proposition 13, and the defeats of Lieutenant Governor Mervyn Dymally and Yvonne Brathwaite Burke for attorney general in the state's elections of 1978 disturbed some California blacks very much. In retrospect, these defeats seem to have been almost inevitable. The climate created by the passage of Proposition 13, which drastically reduced the revenue generated by the property tax, threatened the reelection of Governor Edmund G. ("Jerry") Brown, but his adroit political footwork saved him for a time. The distance that Brown maintained in his relationship with Dymally, the lieutenant governor, when Dymally had his public-relations troubles, stood Brown in good stead but was a blow to Dymally. Furthermore, the lieutenant governor was not able to share in the image of a frugal public official which Brown had adroitly created for himself long before the passage of Proposition 13.

Congresswoman Burke had an equally difficult problem. Her opponent, state Senator George Deukmejian, was the author of a bill favorable to the death penalty which fitted the mood of Californians in that election year. His bill, Proposition 7, won even more handsomely than he did when he defeated the otherwise politically and personally attractive Burke.

These defeats, however, did not seriously impair the visibility of California's other black politicians. Californians continued to see the serene visages of Wilson Riles and Thomas Bradley and the intensity of Ronald Dellums, and they continued to hear the sparkling articulations of Willie Brown. California's political climate would have to undergo drastic and disastrous changes before their presences could be submerged.

Despite the serious defeat of the Democratic party in the 1980 presidential elections, black California officialdom suffered no numerical losses on the national or state levels. The black delegation from California remained four in the House of Representatives, six in the state Assembly, and two in the state Senate—all Democrats. With all of their political eggs in the Democratic party, blacks were vulnerable to the occasional shifts of popular favor. [1]

The state elections of 1982 were indeed a dramatic spectacle of ups and downs for black political figures. On the positive side, the congressional black delegation to the House of Representatives continued to be led by veteran Augustus Hawkins and included Ronald Dellums, Mervyn Dymally (back in public life again), and Julian Dixon, all Democrats and, with the exception of Dellums, from southern California. In the state Senate Bill Greene and Diane Watson were the only black senators, and they, too, were Democrats and also from the Los Angeles area. In the state Assembly, there were six black members, half of them women. They were Teresa Hughes, Gwen Moore, and Maxine Waters, all Democrats and from the Los Angeles area. The three men were Elihu Harris, Curtis Tucker, and Willie Brown. Brown and Harris came from Democratic constituencies in the Bay area that represented largely white voters. Willie Brown's political astuteness and prestige brought him to the Assembly speaker's chair, a most powerful position. In this election, state Superintendent of Public Instruction Wilson Riles lost his bid for a fourth term, thus ending a twelve-year tenure.

Undoubtedly, the most dramatic event of the 1982 state elections was the race between Los Angeles Mayor Thomas Bradley, a Democrat and the city's first black mayor, and George Deukmejian, the state's attorney general and a leading Republican. For many months Bradley was the projected winner. He had a good and popular record as mayor of Los Angeles where the black population was only 17 percent. In November, by a small margin, Deukmejian triumphed over Bradley. The Field Poll organization believed that Bradley lost because he opposed

the gun lobby at a time when a gun-control initiative was on
the ballot and because the Republicans mounted an absentee
ballot campaign that reached new heights.[1] Absentee ballots
are traditionaly heavily Republican. Certain facts are conclusive. Bradley won a majority of the votes of people who walked
or drove to the polls. The absentee ballots of a half million
voters assured Deukmejian the more than fifty thousand votes
by which he beat Bradley. Racism was considered an ingredient
in Bradley's defeat, but how much this can be considered a
factor is murky. Bradley received over 3,750,000 votes, most of
which came from whites. Those interested in demography will
find it instructive to note that a very large majority of Bradley
votes came from urban and coastal counties.

Some months after this election, Bradley gave an intriguing
interview to a reporter from a Stanford University publication
called *Up Front*. The reporter asked this question of Bradley:
"Maxine Waters [Assemblywoman, Los Angeles] said, after the
election, that 'People [blacks] feel, once again, that they have
been rejected by White America.' What would your advice be to
these people? How would you comfort them?" Bradley replied,
"Three million, eight hundred thousand people voted for Tom
Bradley. I think that is comfort enough. What we must realize
is that this was a first time experience and having achieved that
degree of support has been a significant involvement in this
state's political processes."[2]

Despite the defeats of Bradley and Riles in 1982, the Afro-
American presence in California politics is really not diminished. Speaker Willie Brown is constantly in the public eye;
Mayor Bradley had worldwide, favorable visibility as host of the
1984 Olympics. His reelection in 1985 as mayor of Los Angeles
was a smashing victory in spite of weak opposition. That prominence again makes him a potential candidate for governor and
the vice presidency. The state's black delegation to the House of
Representatives in Washington remains four, and in Sacramento
black incumbents of 1982 were reelected in 1984 so that numbers were still two in the Senate and six in the Assembly. In
California, where the black population is about nine percent,
blacks have developed sophisticated alliances with friendly
whites. The coalition politics spurned by black radicals of the

sixties is much admired today by politically active blacks in California and elsewhere in the nation.

A 1980 study based on the federal census revealed a significant trend among upwardly mobile Afro-Americans in the United States — the drift toward the suburbs of the major cities. This is taking place in California as well and is found in the areas of Sacramento, San Jose, Riverside, San Diego, Anaheim, San Francisco, Oakland, and Los Angeles. The strongest of these trends is in the Los Angeles suburbs, which contain 400,000 blacks. The strength of this suburban movement can be measured by the fact that in 1970 over six percent of Los Angeles's suburban population was black and in 1980 close to ten percent. Some of them, one may speculate, have become Republicans as the state gives its majority vote to that party.

The meaning of this trend is clear. When Afro-Americans obtain the means, they wish to better their lives in typical American fashion. However, in terms of individuals this suburban drift among blacks takes on more meaning. While much remains to be analyzed, some details have become available. The major daily newspaper of Los Angeles, the *Los Angeles Times*, undertook, in the late summer of 1982, an investigation of a cross section of articulate Afro-Americans in the Los Angeles area. This study was well done. While the general thrust of the series dealt with the blacks' feelings about living in California of the post–civil rights movement, their past circumstances became part of their responses. A representative number of those interviewed were a part of that census story of blacks in the suburbs. These Afro-Americans, even with their reservations about life in a largely white middle-class community, found much that was quite positive in their new lives. Many felt that the civil rights movement had accomplished a good deal, but they often were guarded about the future and a bit cynical.[3] Their cynicism derived from their belief that the white world was not yet thoroughly reliable in its commitment to progress for blacks. White hypocrisy (real or imagined) was still lurking in the background. For example, the *Los Angeles Times* published a study of minority employees in middle management of corporations. These people felt they were facing a dead end without much hope of entering into real power and money-making opportunities. The series concluded with an excellent and thoughtful editorial entitled "The Black Experience." It read in part:

> Blacks who range in age from 30 to 44 — the generation that came of age during the civil-rights movement — make more money and have better prospects than ever, yet are more distrustful of whites and more pessimistic about the future than blacks older and younger.
>
> Has there, then, been no change?
>
> Blacks are no longer confined to teaching and preaching within the black community or to low-status jobs in the world at large. They range through corporate staffs and university faculties, but not nearly in proportion to their numbers in society. . . . Most fundamentally, blacks and whites simply have more contacts now, in public places and business if not as often socially; acquaintanceship eases understanding. . . .
>
> But it remains an uneasy, distrustful relationship. Many blacks, for example, think that the white-controlled Los Angeles school board's adamant opposition to busing is racism under another name. . . .
>
> Blacks also see some national leaders preach family values and yet seek to restrict money for family planning that would help ease the alarming rate of teen-age pregnancies, especially among blacks. They see a nation not creating enough jobs to give young black men self-respect and money in their pockets.
>
> It remains a time for leadership in the schools, the police department, Congress, the White House — all places where such leadership is little evident today. Blatant Jim Crow racism is gone, but the problems still exist and, being more subtle, may be harder to solve. As black poet James Weldon Johnson wrote, the American racial dilemma "is not a static condition; rather it is, and always has been, a series of shifting interracial situations, never precisely the same for any two generations."[3]

In the meantime, the moods and feelings expressed in the above editorial are undoubtedly being affected by the continued growing impact of Proposition 13. While it gave tax relief to genuine homeowners, it reduced the state's income with the effect of a meat ax that lacked the finesse of the surgeon's scalpel. The difficulties that Proposition 13 placed in the way of cities and counties needing money for fire, police, libraries, and schools meant that these institutions could no longer raise sufficient funds and had to lay off employees. It soon became apparent that schools would be the hardest hit. The largest educational unit of higher education, the community colleges, was particularly stunned. Already a variety of fees has been introduced by the community colleges and tuition is a reality. The alarming predictions of harm are becoming a reality. The press has noted the decline in black enrollment in the community colleges, but it is the decline of opportunity for education for the underclass where the consequences of Proposition 13 are most dramatic. The "Chancellor's Report" presented to the Board of Governors of the California Community Colleges in March 1985 stated that:

> In fall 1983 over 108,000 Black students attended the community colleges, while the next year about 17% fewer Blacks enrolled. Inner-city colleges, which educate the greatest proportion of minorities, suffered the sharpest losses — with some urban campuses losing more than a quarter of their students.

The "Chancellor's Report" revealed a loss in the 1984–1985 enrollment of the Los Angeles Southwest Community College of nearly twenty-seven percent of its minority students. This two-year college is in the heart of the Los Angeles black community. The impact of Proposition 13 was predictable, but sharper upon the minority black students than was even imagined. Barring a reversal of budget cuts, this harmful effect may continue in coming years, even though state budget surpluses have momentarily relieved the pressure of further increases in fees. While the cost of education varies from one community college to another, tuition for a full class load is $50 a semester throughout the state. In addition, books, laboratory and locker fees, and transportation (which may include an automobile) add to the costs of going to school, and may have a severe impact upon those unemployed or living on low wages. The tuition fee thus was the tip of an iceberg when it came to the educational burden.

Nonetheless, black progress in the last two decades in California has been impressive in developing leaders, professional people, scholars, and skilled artisans. More blacks than ever before have become conscious of their future potential. What may prove to be the greatest black victory of the last two decades has been the acceptance by most whites of the belief that life in the United States will be richer and more secure with blacks as full participants.

NOTES

CHAPTER ONE

1. Jack D. Forbes, "Black Pioneers: The Spanish-Speaking Afro-Americans of the Southwest," *Phylon,* XXVII (1966), 241–244.

2. Juan Bautista Alvarado to Allen B. Light, Jan. 22, 1839, Hayes Documents, Part 2, San Diego Archive, Bancroft Library.

3. Zoeth Skinner Eldredge, *The Beginnings of San Francisco* (2 vols., San Francisco: Eldredge, 1912), II, 526–529.

4. Jacob W. Harlan, *California '48 to '88* (San Francisco: Bancroft Co., 1888), 158.

5. *California Star,* Aug. 25, 1847.

6. Charles H. Wesley, *Negro Labor in the United States* (New York: Vanguard Press, 1947), 38, 48; Arthur H. Clark, *The Clipper Ship Era* (New York: Putnam, 1910), 109.

7. Rudolph M. Lapp, *Blacks in Gold Rush California* (New Haven: Yale University Press, 1977), 12–48.

8. *Ibid.,* 166–185.

9. *Ibid.,* 192.

10. *Ibid.,* 210–219.

11. Rudolph M. Lapp, *Archy Lee: A California Fugitive Slave Case* (San Francisco: Book Club of California, 1969), 21–36.

12. Richard H. Orton, *Records of California Men in the War of the Rebellion* (Sacramento: State Printing Office, 1890), *passim.*

13. Charles M. Wollenberg, *All Deliberate Speed* (Berkeley: University of California Press, 1976), 24–25.

14. Forbes, "Black Pioneers," 245.

15. Lapp, *Blacks in Gold Rush California,* 118–125.

CHAPTER TWO

1. *Sacramento Daily Union,* Oct. 25, 1865; *Stockton Weekly Independent,* Jan. 30, 1869; *Elevator,* Jan. 8, 1869.

2. Rudolph M. Lapp, *Blacks in Gold Rush California* (New Haven: Yale University Press, 1977), 92–93.

3. Roy W. Cloud, *Education in California* (Stanford: Stanford University Press, 1952), 45.

4. Charles M. Wollenberg, *All Deliberate Speed* (Berkeley: University of California Press, 1976), 21–24.

5. *Elevator*, March 8, 1873; see also Leigh Dana Johnsen, "Equal Rights and the 'Heathen Chinee'; Black Activism in San Francisco, 1865–1875," *Western Historical Quarterly*, XI (1981), 67–68.

6. *Appeal*, Nov. 24, 1877; March 30, 1878; Feb. 2, 1880; *Elevator*, Oct. 15, 1869.

7. Oscar Lewis and Carroll D. Hall, *Bonanza Inn* (New York: Knopf, 1939), 31, 32, 58.

8. J. Alexander Somerville, *Man of Color* (Los Angeles: Lorrin L. Morrison, 1949), 71.

CHAPTER THREE

1. *First meeting of the Afro-American Congress of California* (San Francisco, July 30, 1895), unpaginated pamphlet in the library of the California Historical Society, San Francisco.

2. *San Francisco Examiner*, July 31, August 1, 3, 23, 1895; June 12, 1896.

3. Eleanor Flexner, *Century of Struggle* (Cambridge, Mass.: Harvard University Press, 1959), 100–101.

4. *San Francisco Chronicle*, Oct. 8, 1896.

5. Louis R. Harlan and Raymond W. Smock, eds., *Booker T. Washington Papers* (Urbana: University of Illinois Press, 1977), 18–25.

6. E. Franklin Frazier, *Black Bourgeoisie* (Glencoe, Ill.: Free Press, 1957), 157–167.

7. Emory J. Tolbert, *The UNIA and Black Los Angeles* (Los Angeles: University of California, Los Angeles, Center for Afro-American Studies, 1980), 27.

8. *Crisis*, II (Aug. 1913).

9. Kenneth Goode, *California's Black Pioneers* (Santa Barbara: McNally and Loftin, 1974), 111.

10. *Colored Directory of the Leading Cities of Northern California, 1916–1917* (Oakland: Tilghman Printing Co., 1916), 3.

11. Charles S. Johnson, *The Negro in American Civilization* (New York: Henry Holt & Co., 1930), 78–79.

12. J. Alexander Somerville, *Man of Color* (Los Angeles: Lorrin L. Morrison, 1949), 125–127.

13. Goode, *California's Black Pioneers,* 89.

14. James A. Fisher, "The Political Development of the Black Community in California, 1850–1950," *California Historical Society Quarterly,* L (1971), 261.

15. Thomas Cripps, *Slow Fade to Black* (New York: Oxford University Press, 1977), 74–89.

16. Quoted in Peter Noble, *The Negro in Films* (London: Skelton Robinson, 1948), 104.

CHAPTER FOUR

1. Lawrence B. de Graaf, *Negro Migration to Los Angeles, 1930–1950* (San Francisco: R. and E. Research Associates, 1974), 86.

2. Lawrence B. de Graaf, "The City of Black Angels: Emergence of the Los Angeles Ghetto, 1890–1930," *Pacific Historical Review,* XXXIX (1970), 327.

3. William F. McDonald, *Federal Relief Administration and the Arts* (Columbus: Ohio State University Press, 1969), 613; Richard Sterner, *The Negro's Share* (New York: Harper and Bros., 1943), 362, 372.

4. Carey McWilliams, *Factories in the Fields* (Boston: Little Brown, 1939), 213; George Ballard Bowers, "Will Imperial Valley Become a Land of Opportunity for Negro Citizens?" *Southern Workman,* LIX (July 1930), 312; Wilson C. Record, *Race and Radicalism* (Ithaca: Cornell University Press, 1964), 95–97, 161–165.

5. Lloyd H. Fisher, *The Harvest Labor Market in California* (Cambridge, Mass.: Harvard University Press, 1953), 24, 48; Bowers, "Will Imperial Valley Become a Land of Opportunity for Negro Citizens?" 312; Wilson C. Record, "The Chico Story: A Black and White Harvest," *Crisis,* LXVIII (Feb. 1951), 95–101, 129–131, 133; Ernesto Galarza, *Merchants of Labor* (San Jose: Rosicrucian Press, 1964), 214.

6. De Graaf, *Negro Migration,* 114–121.

7. Grace H. Stimson, *Rise of the Labor Movement in Los Angeles* (Berkeley: University of California Press, 1955), 336–337; Herbert R. Northrop, *Organized Labor and the Negro* (New York: Harper & Bros., 1944), 207; Robert Weaver, *Negro Labor* (New York: Harcourt Brace, 1946), 173–181.

8. Roger Daniels and Spencer C. Olin, Jr., eds., *Racism in California* (New York: Macmillan, 1972), 266–280.

9. Emory J. Tolbert, *The UNIA and Black Los Angeles* (Los Angeles: University of California, Los Angeles, Center for Afro-American Studies, 1980), 26.

10. De Graaf, "City of Black Angels," 351.

11. *Shelley* v. *Kraemer,* 334 U.S. 1 (1948).

12. W. W. Robinson, *Lawyers of Los Angeles* (Los Angeles: Los Angeles Bar Association, 1959), 168–169.

13. Daniels and Olin, *Racism,* 281–288.

CHAPTER FIVE

1. *Journal of Educational Sociology,* XIX (1945), 166–197.

2. August Meier and Elliott Rudwick, *CORE* (Urbana: University of Illinois Press, 1975), 251–252.

3. Clayborne Carson, *In Struggle — SNCC and the Black Awakening of the 1960s* (Cambridge, Mass.: Harvard University Press, 1981), *passim.*

4. Frederick J. Hacker, "What the McCone Commission Didn't See," *Frontier,* XVII (March 1966), 10–15.

5. Roger Daniels and Spencer C. Olin, Jr., eds., *Racism in California* (New York: Macmillan, 1972), 29–39.

6. Robert Brustein, *Revolution as Theatre* (New York: Liveright, 1971), 13–28.

7. Harry Edwards, *The Revolt of the Black Athlete* (New York: Free Press, 1969), 42–46.

8. *New York Times,* Jan. 5, 1976.

9. Rudolph M. Lapp, *Blacks in Gold Rush California* (New Haven: Yale University Press, 1977), 259.

CHAPTER SIX

1. U.S. Dept. of Commerce, Bureau of the Census, *California* (Washington, D.C.: Government Printing Office, 1970), I, 93; U.S. Dept. of Commerce, Bureau of the Census, *California* (Washington, D.C.: Government Printing Office, 1983), I, Part 6, 104.

2. Lee Rainwater and William L. Yancey, *The Moynihan Report and the Politics of Controversy* (Cambridge, Mass.: Massachusetts Institute of Technology Press, 1967), *passim.*

3. Lawrence de Graaf, "Black Women in the West," *Pacific Historical Review,* XLIX (1980), 305, 307.

4. U.S. Dept. of Labor, Bureau of Labor Statistics, *The Negro in the West* (San Francisco: n.d.), 6, 12, 18, 22, 25.

5. *Black Scholar,* VI (June 1974), *passim* (black family issue); *Crisis,* CXI (Feb. 1984), 12–13.

6. Charles M. Wollenberg, *All Deliberate Speed* (Berkeley: University of California Press, 1976), 158–160.

7. *San Francisco Examiner,* Feb. 28, 1982.

8. *Black Enterprise,* June 1985, 97–105; *San Francisco Examiner.* Oct. 13, 1985, section D; the information on black employees of Motown and Golden State Mutual Insurance company was acquired by telephone interview with the respective personnel departments.

9. *Black Enterprise,* XIV (March 1985), 51–54.

10. *Los Angeles Sentinel,* Aug. 11, 18, 25; Sept. 8, 1983.

11. Roy Ottley, *New World A-Coming* (Cleveland: World Publishing Co., 1945), 320–331.

CHAPTER SEVEN

1. *San Francisco Chronicle,* Feb. 1, 1983.

2. *Up Front* (Stanford: Associated Students of Stanford University, Winter, 1983), 25.

3. *Black Los Angeles: Looking at Diversity* (Los Angeles: Los Angeles Times, 1982), 20, 21. Reprinted as a paperback.

SUGGESTED READINGS

THE RESEARCH AND WRITING of black history in California is still in its early stages of development. The sheer quantity of the materials in the East and the South gives historical writing on the Afro-American experience in these regions a clear advantage. Western materials are much fewer in number and are more deeply imbedded in the conventional sources. This is especially true for the nineteenth century and the first quarter of the twentieh century. The select sources noted in this essay are those which are reasonably accessible.

The first publication of importance that attempts an overview of California black history is the work of Delilah Beasley, *The Negro Trail Blazers of California* (Los Angeles: n.p., 1919). Not written by a trained historian, poorly edited and with many errors of fact, it still stands as immensely useful because of the leads to further research. Beasley interviewed many nineteenth-century families and recorded important materials, much of her information taken from the occasionally faulty memories of old-timers. A more recent survey is Kenneth Goode's *California's Black Pioneers* (Santa Barbara: McNally and Loftin, 1974). There is useful material in Goode's book, but it also contains too much general California history and adds little to knowledge about the period between the gold rush and the 1930s. Jack D. Forbes's *Afro-Americans in the Far West: A Handbook for Educators* (Berkeley: Far West Laboratory for Educational Research and Development, 1969) is a general work with a strong cultural emphasis. Forbes has done research on the pre-gold-rush blacks, and his book is strong in that area, but it also reflects limited research in the 1870–1930 period.

As for special topics, published research in black history is better. Two comprehensive works have recently appeared, which detail educational development: Charles M. Wollenberg, *All Deliberate Speed: Segregation and Exclusion in California Schools,*

1855–1975 (Berkeley: University of California Press, 1976), and Irving G. Hendrick, *The Education of Non-Whites in California, 1849–1970* (San Francisco: R. and E. Research Associates, 1977). Both works include the experiences of other California minorities. The civil rights struggle for a century is discussed in a useful article by James A. Fisher, "The Political Development of the Black Community in California, 1850–1950," *California Historical Society Quarterly*, I (1971), 256–266.

The only comprehensive study of gold-rush blacks is Rudolph M. Lapp's *Blacks in Gold Rush California* (New Haven: Yale University Press, 1977). It describes comprehensively the experiences of this first significant migration of blacks to the West. The book makes abbreviated use of three articles written by the same author: "The Negro in Gold Rush California," *Journal of Negro History*, XLIX (1964), 81–98; "Negro Rights Activities in Gold Rush California," *California Historical Society Quarterly*, XLV (1966), 3–20; "Jeremiah B. Sanderson: Early California Negro Leader," *Journal of Negro History*, LII (1968), 321–333. See also A. Odell Thurman, "The Negro in California Before 1890," *Pacific Historian*, XIX (1975), 321–345, XX (1976), 67–72, 177–188.

In recent years some research has been done on nineteenth-century San Francisco and the Bay area. These works include Francis N. Lortie, *San Francisco's Black Community, 1870–1890* (San Francisco: R. and E. Research Associates, 1973), and James A. Fisher, "The Struggle for Negro Testimony in California, 1851–1863," *Southern California Quarterly*, LI (1969), 313–324. A few unpublished theses for the same period also are noted in the above article by Fisher.

There are no studies of the Negro in California relating directly to the Progressive Era. What limited interest Progressives had in the "color question" was confined to states of the Northeast. Booker T. Washington's visit to California in 1903 and his spectacular reception by whites is at this time debatable as a serious manifestation of Progressivism in racial matters.

The most recent study of blacks in San Francisco, *Pioneer Urbanites* by Douglas H. Daniels (Philadelphia: Temple University Press, 1980), starts with the gold rush era and continues into the modern period. It has much new information and its major thrust is to bring to the reader's attention the social life of blacks, especially those in the middle of the economic ladder. Glimpses of black women in California are provided in Lawrence B. de Graff, "Race, Sex, and Region: Black Women in the American West, 1850–1920," *Pacific Historical Review,* XLIX (1980), 285–313. His citations are especially comprehensive and suggestive of literature in the field.

Twentieth-century materials are more abundant, especially for the period from the 1930s to the 1970s, and for southern as well as northern California. Two excellent pieces by Lawrence B. de Graaf bring Los Angeles black history into sharp focus: *Negro Migration to Los Angeles, 1930–1950* (San Francisco: R. and E. Research Associates, 1974), and "The City of Black Angels: Emergence of the Los Angeles Ghetto, 1890–1930," *Pacific Historical Review,* XXXIX (1970), 323–352. The above article contains substantial bibliographical information in the footnotes. Also valuable are Gail Madyun and Larry Malone, "Black Pioneers in San Diego, 1880–1920," *Journal of San Diego History,* XXVII (1981), 91–114; and Albert Broussard, "Organizing the Black Community in the San Francisco Bay Area, 1915–1930," *Arizona and the West,* XXIII (1981), 335–354. Black migration to the Bay area during World War II is treated in Charles S. Johnson's *The Negro War Worker in San Francisco* (San Francisco: n.p., 1944). A useful article on the same topic is Cy W. Record, "Willie Stokes at the Golden Gate," *Crisis,* LVI (1949), 175–179, 187. Information on discrimination in industry in the West for the same period can be found in Herbert R. Northrup's *Organized Labor and the Negro* (New York: Harper and Brothers, 1944). Also useful are Edward E. France's *Some Aspects of the Migration of the Negro to the San Francisco Bay Area since* 1940 (Palo Alto: R. and E. Research Associates, 1974); and Alonzo Smith and Quintard Taylor, "Racial Discrimination in the Workplace: A Study of Two West Coast Cities During the 1940s," *Journal of Ethnic Studies,* VIII (1981), 34–54.

For students and general readers who wish to pursue more detailed reading on blacks in films and in the film industry, the British cinema historian Peter Noble's *The Negro in Films* (London: Skelton Robinson, 1948) is a fine work. It has a chapter on blacks in British and European films which includes much information about Paul Robeson. However, the most recent and probably most comprehensive study of the American Negro in films and film-making is Thomas Cripps's *Slow Fade to Black* (New York: Oxford University Press, 1977).

With help from the *Reader's Guide to Periodical Literature,* students will find *Ebony* a fruitful source for profiles of many California blacks in public life after 1945. Material on the small town and rural California blacks may exist, but it thus far lies buried in hitherto largely unexamined sources. However, Walter Goldschmidt's *As You Sow* (New York: Harcourt, Brace and Co., 1947), an agricultural study, provides some useful information.

Published material on the post–World War II civil rights revolution and the black nationalist period that followed it is of uneven quality, although in great abundance. Little of it, however, is exclusively devoted to California. The history of the NAACP in the West can be found in the definitive work on CORE by August Meier and Elliott Rudwick, *CORE: A Study in the Civil Rights Movement, 1942–1968* (Urbana: University of Illinois Press, 1973). The book also contains considerable information on the role of CORE in the West. There is some material about SNCC activities in California in the highly acclaimed *In Struggle* (Cambridge, Mass.: Harvard University Press, 1981) by Clayborne Carson. A useful article on Garveyism in the West is Emory Tolbert's "Outpost Garveyism and the UNIA Rank and File," *Journal of Black Studies,* V (1975), 233–253, and his excellent monograph, *The UNIA and Black Los Angeles* (Los Angeles: University of California, Los Angeles, Center for Afro-American Studies, 1980).

Since World War II much has been written on Afro-American history, but material on California blacks during the Depression and the Second World War is fragmentary. In 1972 Daniels and Olin, in their *Racism in California,* wrote that "Despite the vast flood of black studies in recent years, virtually nothing has been done from the historical point of view on the black experience in the Golden State." There has been some improvement in this situation as this section on Suggested Readings indicates. However, in the *Index to Dissertation Abstracts for History, 1973–1982* there are only six completed (but unpublished) doctoral dissertations devoted to California black subjects, two of them done in eastern universities. One of the six, Byron R. Skinner, "The Double V: The Impact of World War II on Black America" (Ph.D. dissertation, University of

California, Berkeley, 1978), has some occasional references to California life.

The Watts riot is dealt with in detail in Roger Daniels and Spencer C. Olin, eds., *Racism in California* (New York: Macmillan, 1972), 281–308. A perceptive and personal view of the riot can be found in the introduction of *From the Ashes* (New York: New American Library, 1967), 1–24, edited by Budd Schulberg. Recent manifestations of black nationalism, such as the Black Panthers, are reported in such works as Reginald Major's *A Panther Is a Black Cat* (New York: W. Morrow, 1971), a sympathetic account which is Bay area–oriented and by a black author. Don A. Schanke's *The Panther Paradox* (New York: D. McKay Co., 1970) is more detached but concentrates on Eldridge Cleaver.

An indispensable tool for scholars of black history in California is James de T. Abajian's *Blacks and Their Contributions to the American West: A Bibliography and Union List of Library Holdings through 1970* (Boston: G. K. Hall, 1970).

In the best traditions of scholarship, varying points of view should be made known to the reader. This is possible where there has been a wealth of writing, but such an accumulation of scholarship does not yet exist for California black history. This new and enlarged edition with much original research must be classified as part of the pioneer work in California Afro-American history. However, where possible, the debatable issues in black history at the national level have been introduced to enable the general reader and student to make judgments and apply them to the California scene.

INDEX